DATE DUE

JAN 3 1 1998	AUG 1 2000
FEB 16 1998	APR 23 '02
MAR 2 1998	MAY 19 '03
MAR 2 1 1998	JUN 2 '03
APR 1 1998	MAY 6 '06
APR 23 1998	MAY 7 '09
MAY 14 1998	OCT 2 '09
	NOV 2 1 '11
JUL 2 0 1998	APR 2 1 2015
JUL 3 1 1998	
AUG 15 1998	
SEP 10 1998	
MAR 29 1999	
APR 26 1999	
JUN 2 8 1999	

CREATING PRIVACY
in the Garden

CREATING PRIVACY
in the Garden

TEXT AND PHOTOGRAPHY BY

CHUCK CRANDALL AND
BARBARA CRANDALL

RIZZOLI
NEW YORK

First published in the United States of America in 1997 by

Rizzoli International Publications, Inc.

300 Park Avenue South, New York, NY 10010

Library of Congress Cataloging-in-Publication Data
Crandall, Chuck.
     Creating privacy in the garden/Chuck Crandall and Barbara Crandall
          p. cm.
     ISBN 0-8478-2003-3 (hc)
     1. Landscape gardening. 2. Garden structures. 3. Screens (Plants) 4. Plants as noise barriers.   I. Crandall, Barbara.   II. title.
SB473.C72 1997
712'.6–dc20   96-44264

Creating Privacy in the Garden
was prepared and produced by
Michael Friedman Publishing Group, Inc.
15 West 26th Street
New York, New York 10010

Editor: Sharyn Rosart
Art Director: Jeff Batzli
Designer: Tanya Ross-Hughes/Hotfoot Studio
Photography Director: Christopher C. Bain
Production Manager: Camille Lee
Illustrations by Oliver Yourke

Color separations by HK Scanner Arts Int'l Ltd.
Printed in Singapore by KHL Printing Co Pte Ltd

Acknowledgments

We would like to give special thanks to our editor, Sharyn Rosart, for her patience and vision in helping us create this magical book. We are also deeply grateful to all the talented garden designers whose creative endeavors can be seen on the following pages, especially Ken Coverdell, Hugh and Mary Palmer Dargan, Michael Glassman, John Herbst, Anne Roth, and Nick and Tree Williams. We would like to thank Becky Bostick of the Hunting Creek Garden Club, the Garden Club of Alexandria, the Garden Club of Fairfax, the Three Chopt Garden Club of Richmond, the Roanoke Council of Garden Clubs, and the Del Mar Garden Club for their unstinting help. Finally, we are indebted to all of the wonderful homeowners, some of whom designed their own gardens, for sharing their charming private out-door spaces with us. They are: Diane Avlon; Commander and Mrs. Bagby; Sandra and Jay Baldwin; Richard and Devon Barkley; Dennice and Richard Beale; Lani and John Berrington; Del and Eugene Blizzard; Norma and Peter Bollinger; Eva and John Breyer; Pam and Gregg Bunch; the Close family; the Cormier family; Roger Cornell; Loretta and Robert Curci; the Dahl family; Caroline and Timothy Dargan; Susan and Ronald Derrow; Bill Ellis, the Ellis-Barnes Garden; the Ferguson family; Virginia and George Francis; the Geurard family; Mrs. George D. Gibson; Kathleen and Michael Glassman; Sue Graham; the Grant family; Irina and Erik Gronborg; Debra and Phillip Haines; Georgianna and Ted Hales; Dr. Ambrose Hampton; Marge and Jack Hawkins; Dr. and Mrs. Hendricks; Cecil Howard and Bob Johnson; the Kay family; Judy Koford and Joe Willis; Maryanne and Bernard Leckie; Marie and Murry Lee; Mario Mathias; Jack and Jennifer Mathis; Patty and Joseph McGee; Mary and Jim McIntire; Jean and Walt Meihoff; the Mellor family; Maryanne and Clinton Morse; Barbara and Anthony Musolino; Cathy and Rick Niemann; Geri and Dick Peterson; Jeanie and Robb Pickens; Valerie and Larry Quate; Peggy and Herb Richards; Captain Phillip and Helen Rush; Michelle and Gary Sackett; the Schibanoff family; Leo Signorotti; the Solomon family; Judy and David Steinberg; the Stevenson family; Tami and Charlie Sutter; the Teichart family; Nancy and Arthur Tesser; Shannon and Byron Tarnutzer; Susan Waggener and Steve McCraken; the Walz family; Wendy Ware and Dan Gleason; Nancy and David Weaver; Patty and Dick Wheeler; and Teresa and Paul Yu.

Contents

Introduction

In my secret garden filled with
Nature's majesty
Tis my private refuge where the
world retreats from me

—John Thomas Giddings

Giddings' heartfelt lines conjure up a poetic vision of something each of us needs from time to time—privacy. Even the most gregarious among us often yearn for seclusion after a day of coping with the demands of modern life and being assailed by a host of exigencies in our workaday world. The garden has long been beloved as a refuge, a place where the experience of greenery, floral beauty, peacefulness, and the cycle of growth replenishes the spirit.

The experience of one garden owner we know is particularly apt. He had worked with a landscape architect to design a large Japanese-style garden with an abundance of natural-looking waterfalls that played almost musically on the ear as you passed by. He had arranged the landscape so that there was no direct access to the front door from the driveway—one had to descend a path to a footbridge spanning a creek, then turn and traverse a long deck to reach the entry. When we asked why the owner chose this meandering approach to his front door, he explained, "Before I come in to greet my wife and kids, I need time to get rid of some of the tension I've brought home with me. I find that this long walk through the garden dispels the stress and rejuvenates my spirit. By the time I go inside, I'm no longer focusing on pressures and problems at the office." For him, the garden provided a transition zone from public to private life. It afforded an opportunity to shed the armor necessary to his business role so that he could enjoy the intimacy of his family.

Privacy means different things to each of us, however, and there are many ways of achieving it.

For many garden lovers, privacy denotes a sensual experience, a chance to fully enjoy a feast for the eyes, ears, nose, and skin, from the sensation underfoot as they step from hard paved surfaces onto lush, green grass to the redolence of scented roses scampering up a pillar. To understand this need, one has only to imagine the soothing splash of water cascading from a fountain and the unrestrained singing of resident birds, the visual feast of color and form in flower and shrub, or the incomparable sweetness of a taste of fresh-plucked strawberries or lettuce.

Our passion for private garden retreats is as old as civilization itself, stretching back across the millennia to the earliest vestiges of Pharaonic Egypt. Murals and scenes on funerary ceramics found in royal tombs depict extensive gardens with walls, pools, floral displays, and trees. High court officials also had their own decorative gardens, but on a smaller scale, since it would not be seemly (or safe) to outdo the pharaoh.

Ramses III was probably the single greatest influence on the establishment of ornamental gardening as a high art form in Egypt, providing funds from his treasury to establish hundreds of temple gardens for worship and pleasure gardens for the diversion of royal advisors and other dignitaries.

We owe our modern concept of the walled garden to various medieval religious sects who surrounded their monasteries with high barriers. This was not done, as one would think, to keep the world and its temptations out, but rather to preclude any distractions. Most of these monastic societies were self-sufficient, growing almost all of their own food in parterre gardens. The Benedictines, for example, were strict vegetarians whose diet consisted of fruit, vegetables, and grains. They and other orders also maintained large medicinal and culinary herb gardens, preserving, expanding, and refining the culture of these useful plants.

Some of these ancient gardens survive today in France and Italy and reveal that, in addition to the purely practical gardens, the monks also established contemplative gardens of roses where they cultivated many old and treasured species thought to be extinct in the secular world.

A generation ago, when families resided for decades in the same house and neighbors were often counted as friends, the trend was to build low fences and walls merely to confine pets and contain children. The erection of high barriers in this "age of innocence" was generally considered a somewhat rude or reclusive act.

But as the twentieth century draws to a close, we have evolved into a teeming, mobile society, and our thinking has begun to change. We seek more privacy from the outside world and yearn for a refuge from the cacophony of the city and pressures of modern life. As we make this transition, we have begun to perceive our gardens not as alien environments, separate from the home, but as integral to our living spaces. Now, we seek ways to incorporate the garden into our personal vision of home.

One result of this new approach is a trend toward "privatizing" the yard. Where codes permit, front yards are being transformed from public spaces into cloistered courtyards that—even though they may front a busy thoroughfare—become secluded havens for family activities.

Backyards are often enclosed with high hedges, fences, or walls and densely planted with barrier shrubs and towering trees to create sheltered retreats and verdant oases. In addition, play spaces, dining areas, and separate garden "rooms" offer discrete spots for each member of the family to find a private realm within the garden.

Creating Privacy in the Garden is your guide to discovering the possibilities and potential in your own outdoor spaces. You will find herein a wealth of new ideas for reclaiming your yard from the chaos of modern life and fashioning it into your own personal paradise.

—Chuck Crandall and Barbara Crandall

CHAPTER ONE

Elements of Privacy

Happy the man whose wish and care
A few paternal acres bound,
Content to breathe his native air
In his own ground

—Alexander Pope

Antique brick walls such as the one shown on the opposite page provide privacy, security, and a convenient structure on which to train climbing plants.

To each of us, privacy has a special meaning. What is private to one person may seem positively isolated to another; for others still, privacy requires a veil but not a barrier.

During our visits to private gardens both here and abroad, we have come across countless interpretations. To an artist, privacy meant being able to step outside into a world that showed no sign of human habitation, where scented groundcover underfoot sent up sweet aromas, and where her eye could discover new floral compositions in the landscape throughout the seasons. She strolled through her garden, she said, to rejuvenate her spirit and to gain inspiration for her work.

An urban couple of our acquaintance who loved city life and their small garden had nevertheless long been disenchanted with the fact that the backyard of their town house was exposed to view from surrounding highrises. They felt as though they were on display whenever they ventured outdoors and yearned for a solution to their life-in-a-fishbowl existence. Their landscape architect designed for them a series of pavilions and plantings that eventually matured into a virtual jungle canopy that effectively shielded them from curious eyes.

Each of us has a personal vision of the ideal private garden space. What is your vision? When you begin to conceive your own private retreat, you'll need to consider how you'll be spending your time outdoors.

Most of us want to be shielded from public view in our outdoor spaces, but there is more to consider in creating privacy. In a city garden, for example, it might be necessary to mute or eliminate intrusive outside noise such as traffic. If you have children, you'll want play areas that are not only fun but also safe and secure. For pets, some method of enclosure will be needed. If your work week requires hectic days away from home, a silent, green nook may be precisely the remedy you seek. Before you begin to create privacy, you must determine what it means to you.

City, suburban, and country gardeners share many of the same goals, and though the space they have to work with may vary considerably, the basic principles in achieving privacy hold true for every kind of space.

The elements of creating privacy fall into three basic categories, which all work in harmony in the quest for a cloistered outdoor retreat. *Structures*, including creatively designed walls, fences, gates, trellises, and screens, can transform an average yard into a beckoning suite of garden rooms where the artwork is provided by nature's master brushstrokes. These versatile structures also shield your garden from view and provide a sense of security in your private world.

Plant material, including hedges, shrubs, trees, and vines, provides shielding greenery and adds drama, color, and perfume. Plants, with their many structural forms and growth patterns, can be called upon to perform other useful functions, including muting noise, providing barriers, screening views into the garden, and masking unattractive sights beyond your property. And of course, the plants are what allow you to create destinations perfect for sitting and contemplating the perfection of a rose or marveling at the complexity and simplicity of the serpentine coil of a vine.

Noise modifiers, such as fountains and other water features, buffer sound while adding music of their own—indeed, the delightful sound of moving water, whether it is a mere rhythmic drip or a boisterous splash, is one of the most soothing sounds in nature's symphonic repertoire, particularly on a torrid summer day. Studies show that the evocative sound of trickling water actually has a cooling effect on us.

Structures

Walls: Beauty and Permanence

Since the earliest civilizations, and probably before, walls have been erected around property to defend it against invaders and miscreants. These sturdy barriers, if well built, frequently survived the structures they were meant to protect. As the threat of invasion waned and towns settled into an agrarian way of life, more decorative walls and fences protected crop and garden plants

Handsome walls such as the restored example, right, and the antique brick one, far right, abound in Charleston, South Carolina, and contribute to the mystique of the city's secret garden district.

from being trampled by wayward animals and children at play.

Among the finest historical examples of residential garden walls, some dating to Colonial America, are those in Charleston, South Carolina, where houses were built cheek-by-jowl and needed a barrier between them for privacy and to obviate property boundary disputes. In today's more urbanized society, walls are raised primarily for the same reasons that prompted those builders of yore to erect their walls.

To a great extent, the materials you use for wall construction will determine the wall's aesthetics. The most common materials are stone and concrete, brick, or cinder block.

Stone is an especially handsome material for walls and is undoubtedly the oldest building material that was readily available to early builders. Over the years, it becomes scaled with lichens and colonized by mosses, giving it a charm and character unrivaled by any other material. A well-constructed stone wall in the right place will endure for many generations. Centuries-old stone may still be seen in the French and English countrysides, as sound and serviceable as the day it were set in place.

Clay brick of hues varying from red to ocher and tan to brown is an elegant material that harmonizes nicely with most architectural styles. As it ages, it takes on a rich patina and beauty, and—unlike stone—it can be painted without diminishing its appeal. Because of its modular dimensions, brick lends itself well to walls of varied design. In addition, bricks can be laid in novel and interesting patterns that add a decorative feature not possible with other materials, such as the serpentine style thought to have been introduced by Thomas Jefferson on returning from Europe, where curved lines in gardens were all the rage. A serpentine wall is sturdier than a conventional wall (Jefferson's is 7 feet [2m] tall and still stands after two

Garden walls are ideal backdrops for quiet retreats, acting as windbreaks and tapestries for nature's artistry while shutting out the intrusions of the city.

hundred years) by the very nature of its shape.

The time, cost, and labor involved in constructing extensive walls have led to the widespread use of blocks and bricks of cast concrete, which are finished with a veneer of half brick, stone, or, more and more frequently, stucco. Because of their size (one block being roughly equivalent in bulk to six bricks) they permit fast, eco-nomical construction of a basic wall. We have seen a concrete block wall 5 feet (1.5m) high and 50 feet (15m) long erected by three masons in a sin-gle day—a feat that could never be du-plicated with brick or stone.

Such walls are well built, yet they lack the intrinsic charm and visual appeal of an aging masonry wall with its interesting patina or a run of stonework with the intriguing play of light and shadow across its surface. However, the creative use of paint and surface textures, greenery, and even fabric can effectively cam-ouflage cinder block, allowing for a truly unique wall statement.

What might have been just another masonry wall be-comes a work of art in its own right when laid in a ser-pentine pattern for visual interest and added strength.

Fences and Gates

Robert Frost, an insightful observer of mankind, wrote, "Good fences make good neighbors."

No society knew more about fences than the eighteenth-century English, who carried their tastes and techniques to their countries of emigration, including the thirteen colonies. For many early settlers, Virginia was a popular destination. In Colonial Williamsburg, now faithfully restored to its 1700s splendor thanks to the beneficence of the Rockefellers, you can see a variety of attractive historical fencing (some 8 miles [13km] of it!), owing to an early town ordinance that required all properties to be enclosed.

Other fine examples of creative fence design are at the George Washington estate at Mount Vernon, Virginia, and Jefferson's magnificent restored plantation, Monticello, near Charlottesville, Virginia, both of which are open for public touring.

In times past, fences were often viewed as temporary solutions to securing the property, while walls were built and hedges and other encompassing plantings matured sufficiently so that artificial barriers could

At right is a whimsical interpretation of ocean waves, a witty touch in a fence that surrounds a beachfront home.

be dispensed with. This thinking has changed somewhat in contemporary times due to economic reality (fences cost far less to build than walls) and innovative fence designs, which can be found in a variety of styles.

Although not as durable and maintenance-free as walls, fences are equally effective as barriers to the uninvited. They are also excellent buffers against wind and street noise and can provide convenient scaffolding for draping climbing plants for vertical landscapes.

If your community has no ordinances governing height, setbacks, and color, you may give free rein to your creative bent in designing fences. A solid panel fence makes a strong statement in terms of both privacy and aesthetics. It allows no viewing in—or out—but the addition of built-in seating, planters, and arbors will visually relieve the monotony of a long fence run. Decorative trim along the top adds architectural interest. Somewhat less intimidating is a solid panel base capped with latticework or alternating panels of lattice, providing air circulation in the garden while offering sites for anchoring climbing roses and vines. A beachfront design that caught our fancy was a double fence that was curved along the entire length of its top to simulate ocean waves.

If the unremitting solidity of such a fence seems too massive and overdone to you, opt for a more open style with spaces between boards or panels, or with lattice inserts to admit breezes and break up the design. To ensure that the gaps do not double as peepholes, you may want to plant layers of shrubs and trees in front of them. Evergreens, obviously, are the best choice—both broadleaf and needleleaf. Some good choices for

this application include arborvitae (*Thuja* sp.), Colorado spruce (*Picea pungens*), deodar cedar (*Cedrus deodara*), and the many varieties of juniper (*Juniperus* sp.) in both shrub and tree form.

If there are local ordinances or other restrictions that prevent you from erecting a fence to the height you desire, plantings of tall-growing shrubs and trees along the interior perimeter achieve the same goal.

Here are two stylish examples of fences that use lattice panels, which admit light and air. The fence at left is tall enough to act as a security barrier as well as a privacy screen.

19

Species like firethorn (*Pyracantha* sp.), holly (*Ilex* sp.), and thorny elaeagnus (*Elaeagnus pungens*) will stand tall and green above your fence—but beware of their punishing thorns.

Some of the most secure and cloistered gardens have as their only protection bastions of high hedges and trees or palisades of thorny, impenetrable shrubs. Greenery can be a potent barrier; planted against walls and fences, it creates an additional buffer against noise, a secondary bulwark against intrusion, and an effective living screen that can, depending upon the species chosen, provide beautiful floral color in season.

Trellises and Screens

With their versatility of design and variety of materials, trellises and screens offer the imaginative garden designer a dizzying array of options. From a traditional fan-shaped trellis festooned with climbing roses in an old-fashioned backyard garden to an inventively draped canvas screen in a rooftop city garden, the design possibilities are limitless.

Loosely defined as vertical structures that may be constructed of wrought iron, lattice, solid wood, or even plastic, trellises provide convenient, portable walls on which to grow climbing plants. For designers, they offer not just plant support, but opportunities to create beckoning private nooks. Within a larger garden, they may be used to divide an expansive space into several smaller garden "rooms." For example, a garden-lover who enjoys dining alfresco might yearn for an outdoor dining nook. Lattice panels could be used to partition off an area convenient to the kitchen. The use of lattice would allow the area to be screened from view, yet the openings between the slats would allow diners to see out

The elaborate Chinese moon gate illustrates the aesthetic purpose of Oriental portals—to frame a beautiful vista that captures the eye and delights the spirit. A vine-covered portico, far right, creates an elegant setting for outdoor dining.

GARDEN PORTALS

A gate is much more than a mere entry to and exit from the garden; it can also make a statement about the people who live beyond. Although the gate is purely utilitarian in function, it is fortunate that few designers throughout history have been able to resist the opportunity to make the gate a decorative—sometimes, even ornate—focal point. The entry gate at the nineteenth-century Wedding Cake House in Kennebunkport, Maine, is a wonderful example of this artistic urge, with its elaborate carving and abundant decorative appliqué.

Many gates are made of openwork and reveal glimpses into the garden that are denied by the surrounding fence. This style, popular among Victorian garden designers, may be a carryover from the European fascination with Chinese moon gates, which caught the fancy of English designers in the last century. Gateways in Chinese gardens are always open and are used as picture frames to surround and present a beautiful view.

Traditional thinking dictates that a gate should harmonize with the style of the fence and the house, but more liberated designers often ignore this rule and create gates that are unique and stand alone as examples of garden art.

Whatever the gate style, it should be wide enough for two adults walking abreast to pass through, or about 4 feet (1.2m) wide.

The hardware for hanging and securing the gate offers another excellent opportunity for imaginative design, but it must also be practical. A gate exerts considerable stress on the posts and hinges that carry its weight—especially when used by children as an impromptu swing. Most gate failures can be traced to hinges that are too flimsy for the task, so this is not a good place to economize.

Probably the most versatile structural element in the residential landscape is the screen, often constructed of lattice as shown on this and the opposite page. Screens do not need to be solid panels to be effective—all of these examples block the view into the garden, permit the flow of air, and introduce dappled shade.

and promote the flow of fresh air (particularly welcome if barbecuing is a favorite cooking method). Climbers, such as wisteria, grapevines, and roses, might be chosen to camouflage the "room" and add a romantic and festive touch.

Low screens and trellises festooned with vines are often used to block direct views into a kitchen garden, or potager, which may not have been designed for viewing and can be somewhat less attractive than the surrounding garden during certain times of the year.

One of the best things about trellises and screens is that when they are judiciously placed, they are invaluable in blocking unappealing views such as utility poles, wires, and other urban visual pollution, as well as unkempt areas in a neighboring yard. For most gardeners, a quick stroll through the garden will reveal these "sore" points in the landscape where a vertical structure might, in effect, wave a magic wand and make the unattractive spot "disappear."

QUICK GROWTH PLANTS FOR SCREENS AND HEDGES

A common desire among many property owners is to find a screening shrub or tree that both grows rapidly and is an attractive addition to the landscape. There are a great many shrubs, as well as a few trees, that offer both these qualities. The trade-off for fast growth is often a shorter life.

Knowledgeable garden designers and landscape architects plan ahead for the eventual demise of temporary screens by starting slower-growing but longer-lived species just in front of "stand-ins." By the time the fast-growth plants begin to deteriorate, the permanent screens are maturing and filling in according to plan.

The following are quick-response shrubs and trees, some of which will survive for decades with optimum growing conditions. Those marked with two asterisks (**) are deciduous.

Acacia baileyana, Bailey acacia (30 feet; 9m)

Acacia longifolia, Sydney golden wattle (20 feet; 6m)

Acer ginnala, amur maple (20 feet; 6m)**

Acer truncatum, Shantung maple (25 feet; 7.5m)**

Bambusa multiplex 'Silverstripe' (25 feet; 7.5m)

Berberis koreana, Korean barberry (8 feet; 2.4m)**

Berberis thunbergii, Japanese barberry (6 feet; 1.8m)**

Carissa macrocarpa, Natal plum (14 feet; 4.2m)

Chamaecyparis lawsoniana, Port Orford cedar (60 feet; 18m)

Cornus stolonifera, red-osier dogwood (15 feet; 4.6m)**

× *Cupressocyparis leylandii*, Leyland cypress (45 feet; 13.5m)

Cupressus glabra, Arizona cypress (30 feet; 9m)

Dodonaea viscosa, hopbush (35 feet; 11m)

Escallonia rubra, escallonia (15 feet; 4.6m)

Eucalyptus species, eucalyptus (V)

Euonymus fortunei, wintercreeper (20 feet; 6m)

Ilex 'Nellie R. Stevens' (18 feet; 5.5m)

Ilex cassine, dahoon holly (20 feet; 6m)

Ilex opaca, American holly (60 feet; 18m)

Lonicera nitida, box honeysuckle (6 feet; 1.8m)

Malus baccata 'Columnaris', columnar Siberian crab apple (25 feet; 7.5m)**

Nerium oleander, oleander (10 feet; 3m)

Philadelphus × *virginalis*, mock orange (8 feet; 2.4m)**

V= Height varies depending on cultivar

ORNAMENTAL SHRUBS FOR HEDGES AND SCREENS

Evergreen shrubs have been used to define property boundaries for centuries and are "friendlier" than walls or fences. While a large number of the shrubs on the following list grow taller, their average height in a residential garden is given. Many of these can be sheared and headed back to produce a more formal, lower-growing hedge, but an equal number are ideal for creating informal hedges. More than a few of those listed have cultivars, or varieties, that are radically different from their parents. Those marked with an asterisk (*) are handsome accent or specimen shrubs that can stand alone as ornamentals. Those marked with two asterisks (**) are deciduous.

Abelia × grandiflora, glossy abelia (10 feet; 3m)*

Acer circinatum, vine maple (25 feet; 7.5m)**

Bambusa glaucescens riviereorum, Chinese goddess bamboo (8 feet; 2.4m)

Berberis buxifolia, Magellan barberry (6 feet; 1.8m)

Berberis darwinii, Darwin barberry (10 feet; 3m)

Berberis koreana, Korean barberry (8 feet; 2.4m)**

Berberis × mentorensis, mentor barberry (7 feet; 2m)

Berberis thunbergii, Japanese barberry (6 feet; 1.8m)**

Buxus microphylla japonica, Japanese boxwood (6 feet; 1.8m)

Buxus sempervirens, English box (20 feet; 6m).

Camellia japonica, camellia species (12 feet; 3.7m)*

Caragana arborescens, Siberian peashrub (20 feet; 6m)**

Carissa macrocarpa, Natal plum (14 feet; 4.2m)*

Chaenomeles speciosa, flowering quince (10 feet; 3m)*, **

Cornus mas, cornelian cherry (7 feet; 2m)*, **

Cornus stolonifera, red-osier dogwood (15 feet; 4.6m)**

Cotoneaster lucidus, hedge cotoneaster (10 feet; 3m)**

Elaeagnus pungens, thorny elaeagnus (15 feet; 4.6m)

Escallonia rubra, escallonia (15 feet; 4.6m)

Euonymus alata, burning bush (10 feet; 3m)*, **

Euonymus japonica, evergreen euonymus (10 feet; 3m)

Euonymus kiautschovica 'Manhattan', euonymus (9 feet; 2.7m)

Forsythia × intermedia, forsythia (10 feet; 3m)*, **

Ilex crenata, Japanese holly (10 feet; 3m)

Juniperus species, juniper (7 feet; 2m)

Ligustrum amurense, amur privet (15 feet; 4.6m)**

Ligustrum × ibolium, ibolium privet (10 feet; 3m)**

Ligustrum japonicum, Japanese privet (10 feet; 3m)

Ligustrum lucidum, glossy privet (30 feet; 9m)

Ligustrum ovalifolium, California privet (12 feet; 3.7m)**

Lonicera korolkowii 'Zabelii', Zabel's honeysuckle (10 feet; 3m)**

Lonicera tatarica, Tatarian honeysuckle (10 feet; 3m)*, **

Mahonia aquifolium, Oregon grape (7 feet; 2m)*

Myrtus communis, myrtle (6 feet; 1.8m)

Nerium oleander, oleander (10 feet; 3m)

Osmanthus fragrans, sweet olive (10 feet; 3m)

Osmanthus heterophyllus, false holly (15 feet; 4.6m)

Philadelphus × virginalis, mock orange (8 feet; 2.4m)*, **

Photinia × fraseri, photina (12 feet; 3.7m)*

Pittosporum tobira, sweet mock orange (8 feet; 2.4m)*

Podocarpus macrophyllus, yew pine (30 feet; 9m)*

Prunus caroliniana, cherry laurel (30 feet; 9m)

Prunus ilicifolia, holly-leaf cherry (25 feet; 7.5m)

Prunus laurocerasus, English laurel (30 feet; 9m)

Pyracantha species, firethorn (10 feet; 3m)*

Rhamnus alaternus, Italian buckthorn (12 feet; 3.7m)

Rhamnus cathartica, common buckthorn (20 feet; 6m)**

Rhamnus frangula 'Columaris', tall-hedge buckthorn (10 feet; 3m)**

Rhaphiolepis indica, Indian hawthorn (6 feet; 1.8m)*

Rhododendron species, rhododendron, azalea (V)

Rosa species, roses (V)

Spiraea prunifolia 'Plena', bridal wreath spiraea (6 feet; 1.8m)*, **

Spiraea × vanhouttei, Vanhoutte spiraea (6 feet; 1.8m)*, **

Syringa vulgaris, common lilac (20 feet; 6m)*, **

Syzygium paniculatum, eugenia (45 feet; 13.5m)

Tamarix aphylla, tamarisk (40 feet; 12m)**

Taxus species, yew (V)

Thuja occidentalis, American arborvitae (V)

Viburnum dentatum, arrowwood (12 feet; 3.7m)**

Viburnum japonicum, Japanese viburnum (20 feet; 6m)

Viburnum opulus 'Compactum', compact European cranberry bush (6 feet; 1.8m)

Viburnum tinus 'Spring Bouquet', laurustinus (12 feet; 3.7m)

Weigela florida, weigela (6 feet; 1.8m)*, **

Xylosma congestum, shiny xylosma (15 feet; 4.6m)

V = Height varies depending on cultivar

A lattice screen draped with Chinese jasmine (*Trachelospermum asiaticum*) delights the senses while shielding the bedroom on the other side from view from the adjacent city street.

Planting for Privacy

Trees

Privacy can often be achieved simply by the judicious placement of layers of shrubs and trees, as shown in the quiet garden corner at right. In urban areas of high density, high fences can be combined with perimeter plantings to create the same effect. Creative fencing, as in the two variations shown at far right, can impart a sense of unique style to the garden.

More than any other element, trees are the backbone of the garden. They add magic and mystery and history—usually attaining their greatest character only after the planter has "shuffled off this mortal coil," having left a living legacy.

Newly set-in trees are investments in the future character of a garden. Scottish poet and avid gardener Alexander Smith was keenly aware of this when he wrote in *Dreamthorp*, "A man does not plant a tree for himself; he plants it for posterity."

Trees are invaluable in the residential landscape for a host of practical reasons, too. First, they improve the quality of the air we breathe by filtering out pollutants and producing oxygen. They moderate the destructive effects of harsh winds on the garden. They shelter us from the torrid summer sun and create nooks for shade-loving plants. They provide a verdant backdrop for understory

plants. Finally, they can offer us a green and living shield in our private outdoor retreats.

Further delights of trees may include, depending on the species chosen, stunning fall color, seasonal floral beauty, the bounty of edible fruits, and winter forage of berries and haws for wildlife.

Unlike most shrubs, which are limited in the height they attain, trees may be used to block overhead views into the garden, a concern for anyone whose private Eden is in the city or densely settled suburb. Indeed, the most often encountered drawback of a garden in the city is that it frequently offers a view to neighbors who live in taller buildings. You can minimize (but probably not completely eliminate) their views with plantings of trees around the perimeter. If you selectively prune the lower branches,

the upper branches will eventually overlap to form a sight-blocking canopy. For permanent screens, choose evergreens such as Douglas fir (*Pseudotsuga menziesii*), eastern red cedar (*Juniperus virginiana*), Leyland cypress (× *Cupressocyparis* sp.), and yew (*Taxus* sp.). For seasonal screens, deciduous types that lose their mantle of foliage during the autumn and winter when the garden is largely unused and may be covered with snow will do fine. Indeed, the sight of their bare, snow-covered limbs reaching out over the garden has its own wintry charm.

TREES FOR SHELTERS, SCREENS, AND BUFFERS

The following is a list of trees that are ideal for garden shelters, screens, and noise buffers. Those marked with two asterisks (**) are deciduous.

Acacia longifolia, Sydney golden wattle (25 feet; 7.5m)
Acer campestre, hedge maple (50 feet; 15m)**
Acer ginnala, amur maple (20 feet; 6m)**
Calocedrus decurrens, California incense cedar (60 feet; 18m)
Carpinus betulus, hornbeam (30 feet; 9m)**
Ceratonia siliqua, carob (40 feet; 12m)
Chamaecyparis lawsoniana, Port Orford cedar (V)
Crataegus monogyna, common hawthorn (30 feet; 9m)**
× *Cupressocyparis leylandii*, Leyland cypress (60 feet; 18m)
Fagus sylvatica, European beech (35 feet; 10.5m)**
Juniperus species, juniper (V)
Juniperus virginiana, eastern red cedar (50 feet; 15m)
Malus baccata 'Columnaris', columnar Siberian crab apple (25 feet; 7.5m)**
Malus sargentii, Sargent crab apple (10 feet; 3m)**
Picea abies, Norway spruce (50 feet; 15m)
Picea glauca, white spruce (60 feet; 18m)
Pinus eldarica, Mondell pine (60 feet; 18m)
Pinus nigra, Austrian pine (45 feet; 13.5m)
Pinus strobus, white pine (80 feet; 24m)
Pittosporum eugenioides, lemonwood (40 feet; 12m)
Pittosporum undulatum, Victorian box (50 feet; 15m)
Podocarpus gracilior, fern pine (30 feet; 9m)
Podocarpus macrocarpus, yew pine (30 feet; 9m)
Populus alba 'Bolleana', bolleana poplar (60 feet; 18m)**
Populus nigra 'Italica', Lombardy poplar (85 feet; 25.5m)**
Populus simonii 'Fastigiata', Simon poplar (50 feet; 15m)**
Prunus lusitanica, Portugal laurel (60 feet; 18m)
Pseudotsuga menziesii, Douglas fir (100 feet; 30m)
Tamarix aphylla, tamarisk tree (40 feet; 12m)**
Taxus species, yew (V)
Tilia cordata, little-leaf linden (50 feet; 15m)**
Tsuga canadensis, Canadian hemlock (90 feet; 27m)
Tsuga heterophylla, western hemlock (100 feet; 30m)

V = Height varies depending on cultivar

Vines and Climbing Plants

With their talent for twining and twisting their way up posts, wires, cables, and the like, vines and climbing plants have been widely used for generations to bring vertical interest to residential landscapes. Some varieties offer additional benefits such as shade or flowers and fruit, making them even more welcome in the garden.

Climbing roses are trained on unobtrusive wire grids across the surface of a wall and trellis to add vertical interest in a tiny space.

Vines can often solve problems that other plants cannot. A family in the Pacific Northwest had a series of decks built in their backyard for outdoor dining and entertaining, but found that even with some tree coverage overhead, the area grew so intensely hot and glaringly sunny as to be virtually uninhabitable on cloudless summer afternoons—the time when they most wanted to be outside. Their landscape architect proposed training vines that would grow up trellises and spread a sheltering canopy of cooling greenery. Since the couple were amateur winemakers, they chose grapevines. Within two years, the vines had matured to the point where they completely covered the trellises and overheads by early summer, then yielded a bountiful harvest of wine grapes before being cut back for the winter.

Ensuring privacy for a spa is another task well suited to vines. Rather than enclosing a hot tub with fencing or walls, which can create a feeling of being boxed in, a better solution may be to install trellising around the spa and cover the structures with broadleaf, dense-growing vining plants like Carolina yellow jessamine *(Gelsemium sempervirens)*, five-leaf akebia *(Akebia quinata)*, passionflower *(Passiflora* sp.*)*, scarlet kadsura *(Kadsura japonica)*, and trumpet creeper *(Campsis* sp.*)*.

Vining plants are excellent choices for use in dressing up an entry, softening the hard lines of a massive wall, or relieving the sterility of a long fenceline. For temporary (or seasonal) screens, there are a number of deciduous or annual vines that offer a fast response, even when planted from seed. Superlative climbers include clematis *(Clematis* sp.*)*, climbing hydrangea *(Hydrangea anomala)*, Dutchman's pipe *(Aristolochia durior)*, grape *(Vitis* sp.*)*, and morning glory *(Ipomoea* sp.*)*. When the season's end signals the loss of foliage, the twisting shapes of the bare vines possess their own distinct visual appeal.

For permanent sight screens, opt for the year-round coverage of evergreen species such as many varieties of English ivy *(Hedera helix)*, Japanese honeysuckle *(Lonicera japonica)*, paper flower *(Bougainvillea* sp.*)*, star jasmine *(Trachelospermum jasmi-*

noides), and wintercreeper *(Euonymus fortunei)*.

The thoroughly romantic look of climbers trained on openwork trellises and arbors, such as those made from lattice, has the benefit of offering an excellent sight screen. For a canopy effect overhead, train vines on wire grids or cables. Four ideal candidates are climbing roses (*Rosa* sp.), grape (*Vitis* sp.), kiwi vine (*Actinidia* sp.), and wisteria (*Wisteria* sp.).

At left, a spa tucked among the trees is screened from neighbors' view by fencing that is softened with climbers that will ultimately camouflage the man-made structure. Boston ivy (far left) *(Parthenocissus tricuspidata)*—a fast-growing climber with striking fall color—creates a mantle of green on these courtyard screens.

CLIMBERS FOR SCREENS

Arctostaphylos uva-ursi, bearberry
Bougainvillea species, paper flower
Euonymus fortunei 'Argenteo-marginata', silver edge wintercreeper
Euonymus fortunei 'Minima', baby wintercreeper
Euonymus fortunei 'Vegeta', evergreen bittersweet
Gelsemium sempervirens, Carolina yellow jessamine
Hedera helix, English ivy
Jasminum species, jasmine
Lonicera japonica 'Halliana', Hall's Japanese honeysuckle
Lonicera japonica chinensis, Chinese honeysuckle
Passiflora species, passionflower
Rosa species, climbing roses
Trachelospermum species, star jasmine

CLIMBERS FOR FENCES

Aristolochia durior, Dutchman's pipe
Bougainvillea species, paper flower
Campsis grandiflora, Chinese trumpet creeper
Campsis radicans, trumpet creeper
Celastrus species, bittersweet
Clematis species, clematis
Hedera helix, English ivy
Ipomoea species, morning glory
Lathyrus odoratus, sweet pea
Lonicera species, honeysuckle
Parthenocissus quinquefolia, Virginia creeper
Parthenocissus tricuspidata, Boston ivy
Phaseolus caracalla, snailvine
Rosa species, climbing roses
Thunbergia grandiflora, Bengal clockvine
Vitis species, grape

CLIMBERS FOR GARDEN WALLS

Bougainvillea species, paper flower
Campsis grandiflora, Chinese trumpet creeper
Campsis radicans, trumpet creeper
Clematis species, clematis
Euonymus fortunei, wintercreeper
Ficus pumila, creeping fig
Hedera helix, English ivy
Hydrangea anomala, climbing hydrangea
Lonicera species, honeysuckle
Parthenocissus quinquefolia, Virginia creeper
Parthenocissus tricuspidata, Boston ivy
Rosa species, climbing roses
Schizophragma hydrangeoides, Japanese hydrangea vine

CLIMBERS FOR TRELLISES, POSTS, AND PILLARS

Actinidia chinensis, kiwi vine
Actinidia polygama, silvervine
Akebia quinata, five-leaf akebia
Aristolochia durior, Dutchman's pipe
Beaumontia grandiflora, herald's trumpet
Celastrus species, bittersweet
Clematis species, clematis
Gelsemium sempervirens, Carolina yellow jessamine
Hibbertia scandens, gold guinea vine
Ipomoea species, morning glory
Jasminum species, jasmine
Kadsura japonica, scarlet kadsura
Lonicera species, honeysuckle
Mandevilla laxa, Chilean jasmine
Rosa species, climbing roses
Schisandra chinensis, Chinese magnolia vine
Trachelospermum species, Confederate jasmine, star jasmine
Wisteria species, wisteria

Water: Nature's Music

Of all the elements in a garden, none is more calming and pleasing to the senses than the presence of water. Whether you prefer the serene surface of a still reflecting pool or the lively spray of a fountain, water introduces a delightfully different element into the garden. It is not merely the sight of water that mesmerizes, but also its sound—and for seekers of privacy, water features mask intrusive noises from without while providing enjoyable sounds within the garden.

The experience of a California gardener whose home was situated near a highway offers an example. Nearly every time he stepped into the yard, he was assailed by the incessant din of traffic. To combat the noise, he enclosed his front entry with a wall to create a private courtyard and, while the wall was being erected, had it plumbed and wired for a cascading water feature. Now he has a secluded entryway where he is greeted by the pleasing splash of water—it is amazing how well the sound of water can muffle harsh noise.

The choices for water features are many, from a minimal Zen pool with a gentle drip to an elaborate stone fountain with spouting mythological figures, and from a natural-looking rock-strewn stream to an ancient-seeming stone urn overflowing into a basin beneath. Whether you prefer the sound of a bubbling fountain or the gentle cascade of a waterfall, the sound will not only soothe the weariest soul, it will also counter most outside noises.

Fountains

A fountain for the garden is an easily installed feature that will soon become an indispensable asset. It may be as simple as a basin with an underwater spout that sends up a light plume or spray of water or as elaborate as a multitiered structure with waterfalls plunging from top to bottom. No matter what type of fountain you choose, it is sure to become a focal point in the landscape, its magical play of water drawing both people and wildlife.

(Note that families with small children should consider a fountain or waterfall without a ground level catch basin, since toddlers are irresistibly drawn to water, sometimes with tragic consequences. Once the children are older, the water feature may easily be upgraded to a larger and more elaborate installation, if desired.)

A grand span of countryside is not necessary for a water feature: for small gardens and city courtyards, there are a myriad of fountain and waterfall designs in scale with these diminutive environments. Many of these are fabricated for mounting on walls with the plumbing hidden inside the masonry. Obviously, these are best installed when the walls are being built, but they can be affixed after construction by competent masons by removing bricks or stones or boring through blocks to insert piping.

Small waterfalls are ideal for garden walls and are no more difficult to set in than a simple fountain, although some thought must be given to designing a fall that produces the desired cascading effect.

The simplest of these wall-mounted features are self-contained with the fountainhead and catch basin as a unit, but many are two-part styles with the fountainhead above and the basin below. These scaled-down versions are extremely popular because of their unobtrusiveness and adaptability to nearly any niche in the garden. Using statues or sculptured figures as spouts can lend an air of whimsy; if the frivolous is not appealing to you, try a minimal effect using an undecorated spout.

Features that introduce the sight and sound of water in a subtler manner are fountains that bubble or drip. These less ebullient—but no less charming—accents are typical of Eastern gardens, many of which have changed little since antiquity.

The Japanese, who absorbed much of their early gardening expertise from China (including the art of bonsai), always include water (or a

At left, a handsome reflecting pool mirrors the sky and lush vegetation that surrounds it, creating a secluded garden oasis. Above, a multilevel fountain with several spouts adds a counterpoint to the songs of resident birds.

Even when it is a mere trickle, the sound of water falling into a catch basin echoes melodically throughout the garden. At far right, a ground-level pool captures images on its surface, adding to the appeal of this garden retreat.

simulation of it) in their gardens. Over the centuries, Japanese gardeners have developed a number of unique water-driven instruments, including the *shishi odoshi*, or boar-whacker, which is designed to frighten wild boar and deer away from prized plantings. It is constructed of bamboo and consists of a pivoting section that fills with water from a stream and, when it is full, drops down and strikes a stone with a resounding clap. It then pivots up again to refill and the process is repeated.

The more elaborate classical Italian and French fountains were once driven by artesian wells, as are the ones at Villa d'Este near Rome. The word "artesian," in fact, comes from the French *artésien*, and means a well dug

deep enough to reach a flow of water that is draining down from higher ground so that the resultant pressure forces the water upward. It is named after the village of Artois, where this type of well formed naturally.

You can re-create the elegant ambience of days gone by with a smaller version of a classically designed fountain, perfect for a more formal garden setting.

FOUNTAIN PLUMBING

Modern fountains and cascades are operated by electrical pumps that force water to the spouting fixture through an outlet pipe or tubing in a continuous recirculating action. Most often used are the noiseless submersible types that are set level in the bottom of the catch basin or pool. These pumps operate on standard household current, consuming no more than would be required to light a 60-watt bulb. Recently introduced are the low-voltage submersible pumps that don't require encasing electrical wires in a conduit to protect them against accidental severing by the garden spade or other mishap. They are wired into a step-down transformer (identical to those used for low-voltage lighting) which is then plugged into a GFI outlet.

Complex fountains with several jets as well as waterfalls with multiple cascades requiring the movement of large volumes of water may call for a surface pump, which is more powerful (and considerably noisier) than the submersible type.

Pools and Ponds

Water in the garden in the form of pools is a distinctly Eastern innovation that probably began with the garden of Pharaoh Amenhotep III (1400 B.C.), whose private retreat boasted four pools containing waterlilies and waterfowl. No culture appreciated the magical, mystical powers of water more, except perhaps the Persians, who often built their gardens around a prominent pool. Cyrus the Great's garden at Persepolis was said to have contained several large pools.

Ornamental pools and ponds, with or without moving water, provide a serene retreat in cloistered gardens. Placid pools containing aquatic plants, fish, and other animals (aquatic snails, frogs, etc.) soon become self-sufficient ecosystems supporting a complex world in microcosm. The interplay of light and shadow, the flashes of color as fish break the surface, and the exotic beauty of lotuses, lilies, and other plants as they come into bloom provide endless hours of enjoyment and fascination.

Pools are classified as "formal" or "informal" depending upon their configuration. To be classified as

For nature lovers, a self-sustaining ecosystem, as shown above, is the ultimate paradise. This pool is full of aquatic life, including frogs, fish, dragonflies, and plants that prosper in and around aquatic environments. A recirculating fountain adds the delightful splash of moving water.

formal, pools must be circular, oval, square, rectangular, or a balanced combination of these forms. An informal design is one of irregular or free-form shape and is often conceived to mimic natural pools and small ponds that occur fortuitously in the wild landscape. Generally, formal pools are placed in formal gardens, especially in cases where the adjoining house is of classic architectural style. Informal pools and ponds are often designed for suburban and country settings with corresponding garden styles, such as cottage gardens. Monet's pond at Giverny is a fine example of informal naturalness, while Louis XIV's elegantly conceived water feature at Versailles typifies the rigidly formal.

Informal pools are traditionally stocked with a balanced selection of aquatic plants as well as fish and other animals. These enhancements may or may not be used in formal pools, in which the reflecting quality of the water or the soothing sight and sound of moving water is sufficiently sublime.

Contrary to what you may imagine, pools and ponds teeming with aquatic life are virtually self-sufficient, if the proper balance among plants, animals, and water volume is maintained. Fish should not be thought of as pets requiring feeding and maintenance—unless one is keeping the aristocratic Oriental koi carp or hi-goi carp, which require regular feedings of high-protein foods. Goldfish and other species do appreciate an occasional feeding of specially formulated food, but can easily sustain themselves on the plant life and algae in the pool.

Wildlife Way Stations

For a great many people, a significant part of enjoying the garden comes from sharing it with the birds, butterflies, and other creatures that are drawn to the bounty of nature concentrated in the average garden. Many nature lovers go to considerable lengths to create a safe, sequestered haven for wildlife within the garden. Habitats that attract desirable visitors are easily created by the addition of irresistible lures such as food, water, and shelter.

Food does not have to mean feeders. Natural sources of nourishment for birds, butterflies, and squirrels come from a variety of fruit-, nut-, seed-, and flower-bearing plants (see sidebars). In wintertime, however, you may wish to add feeders well stocked with seed, suet, and other treats to supplement the meager forage available to wildlife then.

If you do decide to use bird feeders, you should note that the activity this creates will often attract neighborhood cats to the area who will stalk their avian prey with a vengeance and disturb plants and beds while relieving themselves. Once these feline interlopers are

drawn to the garden, it is difficult to discourage future incursions.

Water may be offered in a strategically placed birdbath or pond in open areas of the garden. These are especially beneficial during the summer, when natural water sources may have dried up.

In recent years, shelter for birds has come to mean birdhouses, and these have proliferated in gardens throughout the world. Few of these man-made domiciles are actually inhabited by birds (with the exception of bluebird boxes), but they are colorful ornaments for the garden. Birds generally prefer tall trees with heavy canopies of foliage where they can build their nests in relatively safe, hidden niches.

At left, colorful and friendly koi rush to be hand-fed. Above, a tropical wonderland that has been created not in some exotic location, but in a backyard in the heart of Los Angeles, California. Its forage and evergreen foliage attract a variety of birds native to the L.A. basin.

SHRUBS (nectar or fruit for birds)

Aronia arbutifolia, chokeberry
Callicarpa bodinieri giraldii, beautyberry
Carissa macrocarpa, Natal plum
Cestrum nocturnum, night-blooming jasmine
Chaenomeles species, flowering quince
Cornus mas, cornelian cherry
Cotoneaster species, and cultivars, cotoneaster
Elaeagnus commutata, silverberry
Garrya elliptica, silktassel
Ilex species, holly
Kolkwitzia amabilis, beauty bush
Ribes species, currant, gooseberry
Vitis species, grape
Weigela species and cultivars, weigela

TREES (fruit or seed for birds)

Abies species, fir (V)
Amelanchier laevis, serviceberry (40 feet; 12m)**
Arbutus unedo, strawberry tree (35 feet; 10.5m)
Betula species, birch (V)**
Carpinus caroliniana, American hornbeam (30 feet; 9m)**
Celtis occidentalis, common hackberry (50 feet; 15m)**
Crataegus species, hawthorn (V)**
Fagus sylvatica, European birch (65 feet; 19.5m)**
Larix species, larch (V)**
Malus baccata, crab apple (V)**
Morus species, mulberry (V)**
Picea species and cultivars, spruce (V)
Pinus species, pine (V)
Prunus species, cherry (V)**
Quercus species, oak (V)**
Sorbus species, mountain ash (V)**
Ulmus species, elm (V)**

V = Height varies depending on species, cultivar
** Both evergreen and deciduous depending on species

PERENNIALS AND ANNUALS (nectar or seed for birds)

Ageratum houstonianum, flossflower
Antirrhinum majus, snapdragon
Aquilegia species and cultivars, columbine
Campsis radicans, trumpet creeper
Coreopsis species, coreopsis
Cosmos bipinnatus, cosmos
Delphinium species and cultivars, delphinium
Digitalis species, foxglove
Helianthus annuus, common sunflower
Heuchera species and cultivars, coralbells
Lobelia cardinalis, cardinal flower
Lonicera species, honeysuckle
Mimulus species, monkey flower
Monarda didyma, bee balm
Nicotiana alata, flowering tobacco
Penstemon species, beardtongue
Phlox species, phlox
Tagetes species, marigold

MISCELLANEOUS PLANTS (nectar for butterflies)

Abelia × *grandiflora*, glossy abelia
Ageratum houstonianum, flossflower
Allium species, chives
Allium species, ornamental allium
Arabis species and cultivars, rock cress
Asclepias tuberosa, butterfly weed
Aster species, aster
Buddleia species and cultivars, butterfly bush
Coreopsis species, coreopsis
Cosmos bipinnatus, cosmos
Echinacea purpurea, purple coneflower
Echinops exaltatus, globe thistle
Helenium autumnale, common sneezeweed
Heliotropium arborescens, common heliotrope
Hesperis matronalis, dame's rocket
Lavandula species and cultivars, lavender
Lilium species and cultivars, lily
Limonium species and cultivars, statice
Lonicera species, honeysuckle
Lunaria annua, money plant
Lysimachia punctata, loosestrife
Monarda didyma, bee balm
Myosotis species, forget-me-not
Nicotiana alata, flowering tobacco
Phlox species and cultivars, phlox
Physostegia virginiana, obedient plant
Prunus species, cherry
Rhododendron species and cultivars, rhododendron
Rudbeckia hirta, gloriosa daisy
Scabiosa species, pincushion flower
Syringa species, lilac
Verbena species and cultivars, verbena
Zinnia species, zinnia

Planning Your Private Eden

Now that you have defined privacy for yourself, having carefully considered current and possibly future problems of lack of privacy, unappealing views, sun, wind, and noise sources, you are ready to plan your own private Eden.

To help you envision your plan and bring into clearer focus the design solutions described in this chapter and throughout the book, a number of actual, successfully executed garden plans appear in Chapter Six: Redesigning the Garden. You may find elements of these garden designs adaptable to your space, or you may want to start fresh—in either case, you'll look forward to the luxury of a private garden.

This mature garden, the result of many years of planning and hard work, offers the resident family many areas for their outdoor activities, ranging from a flat plane for children's games to a private, terraced woodland retreat for exploration and bird-watching.

CHAPTER TWO

The Front Yard—a forsaken resource

Gardens are for people—for people
to live in and work around as well
as for them to gaze at.

—Thomas Church, *Your Private World*

Many families who have bought a home in the last decade have experienced the phenomenon known as "the shrinking lot." Developers, eager to maximize their investment, began to whittle down lot sizes to half or less than half the square footage that was once considered minimally acceptable. This trend has increased the density in most new communities and additions to a point where one can, whether one chooses to or not, learn more about the neighbors' private lives than one might care to know.

Those homeowners who feel passionately that the home should be a bastion against an encroaching world

will often go to considerable expense and inconvenience to achieve privacy in their outdoor spaces, unwilling to cede an inch of it.

In response to the shrinking lot sizes, landscape architects and designers began the previously almost unheard-of practice of erecting walls and fences around city front yards, prompting a few raised eyebrows among residents, although as a goodwill gesture neighbors on either side usually had been consulted before work commenced. After all, they would be living with (perhaps even benefiting from) the proposed new barrier.

With the exception of a few estates and special gardens and some upscale sections of cities (such as most of San Marino, California), the residential front yard has historically been a quasipublic space, exposed and violable. Any door-to-door salesman, solicitor, or distributor of advertising broadsides had access to the front door—it was the American way. As a gesture of friendliness we have always made ourselves available to neighbor and stranger alike.

Before the advent of television, and during a time when people lived less in each other's pockets, there was a tradition that was called "going visiting," which is now only a dim memory in American folklore. After the evening meal, families would gather on their front porch (now designed out of contemporary architecture as passé) and either greet their neighbors strolling by or join them in their promenade.

Today, these traditions have for the most part been lost, and in a world in which people are packed ever more closely together, a certain aloofness from one's neighbors has become more acceptable. In recent years, reclaiming one's front yard for private family use has become a burgeoning trend. It is predominantly an urban phenomenon, growing out of a yearning for privacy and a need for security. City lots are woefully Lilliputian and the front yard is often the only outdoor space of any consequence.

Such was the case of one family who built their home on a lot that sloped in the rear into a ravine. While the views out their back windows were breathtaking, there was little rear yard access for a children's play area or entertaining—so they looked to their front yard for a solution. Enclosed by a wall and paved over, with the exception of planters and perimeter bed areas, it became a blank slate for their creativity. By adding seating, a fountain, and a selection of potted and bedded plants, they created a front-yard oasis. Since their house was masonry, they wisely chose to use brick of the same type for their courtyard floor. To relieve the visual impact of an unbroken mass of masonry, they installed openings for planters and filled these with shrubs and trees. They had a seating bench built for themselves that extended the length of the front facade and stained it the same color as the house trim. They filled the facade with colorful pillows covered with durable canvas.

In an out-of-the-way corner, they installed a sandbox with an adjoining playhouse for their preschool children, with an eye toward converting the space to other uses as the youngsters grew older.

Finally, the addition of two festive market umbrellas, a patio table and seating, and a pair of chaises transformed what was once a sterile, exposed front yard into an extension of their private space, a popular destination for the family and a useful venue for parties.

At left one of the myriad courtyard gardens in the charming historic section of Charleston, South Carolina. Here, the homeowners have retrieved private outdoor space from an unlikely spot—the front yard—in an area of tightly-packed homes where land is too scarce for large gardens.

Achieving privacy in the city front yard is a challenge, yet these two families solved the problem with style. Right, landscape plantings are used to good effect to conceal the yard and its occupants. The wall, far right, has a sculptured feel. Fronted by a curbside garden, it creates a welcoming yet totally private entry.

42

Creating Privacy at the Curb

*I*t is often impossible to achieve total privacy in an urban front yard, but there are a few tricks that can at least veil your activities from public scrutiny and allow you to choose your own view rather than look at what your neighbors have wrought.

In many cities, it is possible to build or plant on the property line at the public sidewalk; other communities require a setback. Also, some ordinances permit you to plant up to the property line, but prohibit erecting structures such as walls and fences. A phone call to your local building department will let you know what restrictions, if any, exist in your area.

Don't despair if permanent barriers are forbidden along the property line—they can be equally effective closer to the home. And there is usually no regulation that prevents planting against the streetside of the wall or fence, so you can add a second barrier by putting in tall-growing evergreens. This technique is particularly useful when local regulations restrict the height of residential fences.

If you want your planting to present a formidable physical barrier as well as a visual one, the most effective of the barrier shrubs are those with thorns, spikes, and spiny foliage. Two of the best of these offer bonus features, such as the summer-blooming floral clusters of the firethorn (*Pyracantha* sp.), which are followed by red or orange berries in late summer and fall that persist through the winter, and the bright red fruit and golden variegated foliage of the golden elaeagnus (*E. pungens* 'Maculata').

BARRIER HEDGE PLANTS

Berberis species, barberry
Carissa macrocarpa, Natal plum
Carpinus betulus, hornbeam
Chaenomeles speciosa, flowering quince
Crataegus species, hawthorn
Elaeagnus pungens 'Maculata', golden elaeagnus
Ilex species, holly
Mahonia aquifolium, Oregon grape
Pseudotsuga menziesii, Douglas fir
Punica granatum, pomegranate
Pyracantha species, firethorn
Rhamnus cathartica, buckthorn
Rosa species, rose
Taxus species, yew

A masonry wall of unique design, above, is a charming yet effective barrier. Far right, a substantial curbside wall and handsome wrought iron gate make an elegant statement.

It may also be possible to plant shielding trees if there is a median strip between the curb and sidewalk. Although this is usually considered city property, some municipalities permit homeowners to landscape and maintain these areas. Check with your city planning department to learn what restrictions apply.

For year-round screening, select either broadleaf or needle-leaf evergreens, but be aware that evergreens will also block light in winter, which could result in a darker, drearier yard than you would like. Since the space is likely to be used less during the winter, a wiser choice would be to mix in deciduous material so that some light and winter sun can filter through.

What if your home sits rather closer to the street than would allow for the planting of your own forest twixt house and avenue? One option is to erect screens or hedges very close to the house. For a country-in-the-city look, you might try lattice sections on which evergreen vines are trained. A more solid fence up against the house could also be softened with greenery. Either type of structure could be buttressed with a row of evergreen shrubs or small trees, such as English box *(Buxus sempervirens)*, intermediate yew *(Taxus × media)*, juniper *(Juniperus* sp.), or waxleaf privet *(Ligustrum japonicum)*. Residents of mild-winter regions may also consider citrus *(Citrus* sp.), hibiscus *(Hibiscus rosa-sinensis)*, and myrtle *(Myrtus communis)*.

One family solved the problem of headlights piercing street-facing bedrooms at night by erecting a series of screens a few feet in front of the windows and training climbing plants on them. This blocked the invasive shafts of light from passing traffic but admitted natural light and allowed outward views.

Courtyard Entrances

A courtyard is far and away the best solution for transforming an exposed front yard into a private, secure outdoor room. When codes permit enclosing the space out to the sidewalk, the benefit is even greater, as described earlier, providing newfound space for all sorts of uses, from entertaining to play areas for children and adults alike.

Most courtyards are walled or fenced, but—as previously discussed—in communities where man-made barriers are forbidden or restricted as to height or setback limitations, plantings may be equally effective in creating a private front-yard domain. Note, however, that fences and hedges cast shade on the neighboring yards, causing a decline in the lawn or shrubs growing there. Also, when hedges are planted on the property line separating you from a neighbor, it is important to note that some species require regular pruning and shaping to maintain their handsome appearance. Formal hedges of box (*Buxus* sp.), cherry laurel *(Prunus laurocerasus)*, and yew *(Taxus* sp.), for example, need tending on your neighbor's side, as well. For this reason, in the interest of

This splendid gate breaks up the solid wall and provides just a glimpse into the courtyard garden for visitors and passersby.

The gate provides a wonderful opportunity to express yourself. It's the first thing approaching visitors will focus on and it literally frames the view into the garden—what better place to make a statement about the style of the garden and the people within? For an artist couple we know, the opportunity was irresistible. They designed their entry gate as a whimsical interpretation of the American flag—a colorful and patriotic hint of the playful accents that await guests in the courtyard and garden beyond.

In lieu of transforming the entire front yard into an enclosed outdoor room, you may elect to turn a portion of it into a smaller, closed-off area to create a private entranceway. If you want to use the space for other activities, there are many options—consider a patio accessible through French doors for intimate dining or a secluded corner walled off from the front door, perfect for curling up with a book.

This was the solution chosen by a couple who has ample flat lawn area in their front yard but no space where they could enjoy a private moment when they ventured out. They contracted to have a large patio installed in a portion of what had been lawn, and had a wall built that matched the material used on the exterior of the front elevation (stucco and brick) to enclosed this retreat. A side wall was opened to accommodate double French doors that open onto this new outdoor room, which the couple uses several times a year for garden parties and even more often for intimate, leisurely Sunday brunches.

For a private outdoor foyer, extend the hardscape used in the entry walk into the new sanctuary. To emphasize the feeling of emerging into a

A novel gate, left, designed by the artist couple who own the home, sets the mood for a stroll through the garden beyond filled with sculpture and capriccios. Below, a gate adorned with hand-tooled beach grasses gives a seashore home a unique and inviting entrance.

harmony, it is a good idea to consult with neighbors before presenting them with a fait accompli that inflicts new garden chores on them.

A gate will be the focal point of the courtyard entrance. Solid gates of wood or metal provide the most privacy, but if this is not of paramount importance, wrought iron and open-work gates of wood offer the same level of security but are much more interesting visually. They also allow you to observe visitors and open the yard up to cooling breezes.

Two examples of courtyard gardens are seen on this and the opposite page. Right, a lavishly planted wall conceals the garden beyond, while generous stairs lead up to gates that harmonize architecturally with the courtyard design. Far right, encircling containers of color focus the eye on the heroic sculpture.

different space, you might instead lay a floor of brick or flagstone. For a more verdant look, try a curving arrangement of stone pathways edged by ground cover.

For even greater seclusion, add a "roof" of lattice or other openwork on which vining plants may be grown to create a cozy loggia for outdoor repasts and relaxation.

A less ambitious solution is to simply install a short section of fencing or a row of shrubs or small trees, such as eugenia *(Syzygium paniculatum)*, juniper *(Juniperus* sp.), or English box *(Buxus sempervirens)*, that create a screened-off portion of the yard hidden from view. One family accomplished their goal of taking back some of their exposed front

yard for private use by fashioning a U-shaped enclosure out of sturdy barn-wood planters in which they grew boxwood hedges. These portable screens, equipped with wheels, can be easily moved to form other configurations. By combining planters with portable trellises, you could easily create a movable private alcove.

The Front Porch

The front porch was once an elevation ideal for watching the world and being watched. Today, most of us prefer to enjoy our outdoor time alone or with family members, rather than interacting with neighbors or passersby. Since many front porches were built back in that other, more outgoing era, you may have wished for some imaginative solutions to help screen your porch from the world without converting it to an indoor room.

A porch is, however, the ideal setting for creating a private *outdoor* room, despite the fact that it may front on a busy street or may have only a skimpy setback. There are a number of ways this can be accomplished—with porch boxes and planters filled with shade-tolerant shrubs and trees; with lush hanging baskets and planters brimming with annuals, perennials, and trailers that prosper in low light levels; with roll-down shades and awnings that shield a portion of the space from view; and by employing trellises or lattice panels on which you train vining and climbing plants.

Right: Lush growth and strategic plant placement combine to create privacy. Far right: Screens surrounding and overhead created this quiet dining enclave, which is softened by greenery at every level. The play of light through the screens adds visual interest.

A cool, shady retreat on a hot summer day, the front porch is still one of the most useful and popular outdoor rooms. By strategic placement of potted and hanging plants, you can create a dense screen of greenery, or, as in this charming example, a simple softening of the architecture.

PLANTS FOR PORCH GARDENS

Bulbs, Corms, and Tubers
Begonia × *tuberhybrida*, tuberous begonia
Caladium × *hortulanum*, caladium
Clivia miniata, Kaffir lily
Convallaria majalis, lily of the valley
Cyclamen species, cyclamen
Leucojum species, snowflake
Scilla species, squill, bluebell

Annuals (including perennials grown as annuals)
Begonia × *tuberhybrida*, bedding begonia
Browallia speciosa, amethyst flower
Campanula, bellflower
Clarkia species, godetia
Coleus × *hybridus*, painted nettle
Euphorbia marginata, snow-on-the-mountain
Impatiens balsamina, balsam
Impatiens wallerana, busy lizzie
Mimulus species, monkey flower
Myosotis sylvatica, forget-me-not

Nicotiana alata, flowering tobacco
Torenia fournieri, wishbone flower
Tropaeolum majus, garden nasturtium
Viola hybrids, violet, pansy

Perennials
Anemone species, windflower
Aruncus dioicus, goatsbeard
Astilbe hybrids, false spiraea
Brunnera macrophylla, brunnera
Digitalis purpurea, foxglove
Dryopteris species, wood fern
Hosta species, plantain lily
Mertensia virginica, Virginia bluebells
Polygonatum species, Solomon's seal
Polystichum species, shield ferns
Primula malacoides, fairy primrose
Primula × *polyantha*, polyanthus primrose
Primula vulgaris, English primrose
Pulmonaria saccharata, Bethlehem sage
Tradescantia virginiana, spiderwort

Shrubs and Trees
Acer palmatum, Japanese maple
Aucuba japonica, Japanese aucuba
Camellia japonica, Japanese camellia
Camellia sasanqua, sasanqua camellia
Cornus florida, flowering dogwood
Euonymus fortunei, wintercreeper
Fatsia japonica, Japanese aralia
Ficus benjamina, weeping fig (frost-tender)
Ficus elastica decora, rubber tree (frost-tender)
Ficus microcarpa (F. retusa), Indian laurel fig (frost-tender)
Hamamelis × *intermedia*, witch hazel
Hydrangea macrophylla, big-leaf hydrangea
Kalmia latifolia, mountain laurel
Leucothoe fontanesiana, drooping leucothoe
Ligustrum species, privet
Mahonia species, mahonia, Oregon grape
Osmanthus fragrans, sweet olive
Osmanthus heterophyllus, holly olive
Podocarpus species, fern pine, yew pine (frost-tender)
Rhododendron species, azalea, rhododendron
Taxus, yew

Planting for Privacy

Screening Plants

Broadleaf and needle-leaf evergreen shrubs and dwarf trees are the best choice for screens, since they perform the task of shielding private spaces year-round. In addition to the ones mentioned above, some of the best of these for screening applications follow.

Living walls of evergreen plants are among the most effective privacy-enhancing plantings. The inset photo, far left, shows a small bedroom patio sheltered from view by a wall of climbers.

SCREENING PLANT	HEIGHT	SPACING IN 5 YEARS
Cupressocyparis leylandii Leyland cypress	4–8 feet; 1.2–2.4m	12–20 feet; 3.7–6m
Elaeagnus pungens thorny elaeagnus	4–6 feet; 1.2–1.8m	8–10 feet; 2.4–3m
Ilex × attenuata 'Fosteri' Foster holly	4–8 feet; 1.2–2.4m	8–10 feet; 2.4–3m
Ilex × attenuata 'Savannah' Savannah holly	6–8 feet; 1.8–2.4m	8–10 feet; 2.4–3m
Ilex cornuta 'Burfordii Nana' dwarf Burford holly	3–4 feet; 1–1.2m	5–6 feet; 1.5–1.8m
Ilex × 'Nellie R. Stevens' 'Nellie R. Stevens' holly	6–8 feet; 1.8–2.4m	10–12 feet; 3–3.7m
Juniperus chinensis 'Pfitzerana' Pfitzer juniper	6–8 feet; 1.8–2.4m	6–8 feet; 1.8–2.4m
Juniperus chinensis 'Spartan' upright juniper	4–6 feet; 1.2–1.8m	14–18 feet; 4.2–5.5m
Pinus thunbergiana Japanese black pine	8–12 feet; 2.4–3.7m	7–12 feet; 2–3.7m
Taxus cuspidata 'Nana' dwarf Japanese yew	3–4 feet; 1–1.2m	5–6 feet; 1.5–1.8m
Tsuga canadensis 'Compacta' dwarf Canadian hemlock	3–4 feet; 1–1.2m	3–4 feet; 1–1.2m

Social Climbers

Climbing and cascading plants are all too often overlooked in the landscaping scheme, yet these vigorous vines and trailers are valuable, colorful assets. They can cover a vertical structure, relieve the monotony of a blank wall, and provide a blanket of colorful and often scented blooms that last through the summer.

Although some are slow-growing, permanent residents of the garden, others are fast-response annuals that offer a season of bold color to brighten an entry or adorn a pillar. They are useful summer cover-ups that must be started anew each spring from seed, although some self-sowing types once established renew themselves. This talent may not always be an admirable one in some invasive species, such as morning glory (*Ipomoea* sp.).

Most climbers and twiners are either deciduous or are perennials treated as annuals in cold-winter climates, but there are some winter-hardy evergreens—the many handsome cultivars of both English ivy (*Hedera helix*) and wintercreeper (*Euonymus fortunei*), for example. In areas devoid of winter frosts and freezes, the list of vining options increases twentyfold, since most vines originated in the temperate subtropics.

Some of the best climbers and twiners for the home landscape with their floral color (if any) noted follow.

While each outdoor space is unique and every family's needs are different, the inventive solutions for reclaiming one's front yard outlined in this chapter are adaptable, at least in part, to any yard—including yours.

Fences can be softened with vines or, as shown in the photo at far left, cascaders such as weeping atlas cedar *(Cedrus atlantica* 'Pendula'*)*. Walls may also be "landscaped," as seen in the photo at left, which shows a tapestry of honeysuckle, ivies, and climbing rose.

57

Vining plants have a captivating knack for clambering up and over structures and cloaking them with a mantle of green. At right is a Colonial-era brick garden tool storage outbuilding covered with Lady Banks'rose *(Rosa banksiae).*

Perennials

Akebia quinata, five-leaf akebia (lavender)

Campsis radicans, trumpet creeper (red, yellow)

Campsis × tagliabuana 'Mme Galen', Mme Galen trumpet creeper (red)

Celastrus scandens, bittersweet (white)

Clematis texensis, scarlet clematis (scarlet)

Euonymus fortunei, wintercreeper

Hedera helix, English ivy

Hydrangea anomala, climbing hydrangea (white)

Lonicera japonica 'Halliana', Hall's Japanese honeysuckle (white, yellow)

Lonicera sempervirens, Japanese honeysuckle (yellow)

Menispermum species, moonseed (white, yellow)

Parthenocissus quinquefolia, Virginia creeper

Parthenocissus tricuspidata, Boston ivy

Rosa banksiae, Lady Banks rose (white, yellow)

Rosa laevigata, Cherokee rose (white)

Schisandra chinensis, Chinese magnolia vine (white, pink)

Annuals

Asarina scandens, chickabiddy (white, pink, dark blue)

Dolichos lablab, scarlet runner bean (scarlet)

Ipomoea alba, moonflower (white)

Ipomoea tricolor, morning glory (many colors and combinations)

Mina lobata, exotic love (creamy white)

Quamoclit pennata (Ipomoea pennata), cypress vine (cardinal red)

Thunbergia alata, black-eyed Susan vine (orange, yellow)

Thunbergia grandiflora, Bengal clockvine (light blue)

Cascaders

Bougainvillea species, paper flower (mostly reds)

Cotoneaster hybrids, cotoneaster (white, pink)

Gelsemium sempervirens, Carolina yellow jessamine (yellow)

Pyracantha species, firethorn (white)

Rosmarinus officinalis, trailing rosemary (pale lavender)

Wisteria species, wisteria (white, pink, lavender)

Top left, an entry screen and planter provide a handsome framework for fast-growing evergreen clematis *(C. armandii)*, which bears showy white blooms in early spring. Top right, a combination playhouse and garden storage room is festooned with blood red trumpet vine *(Distictis buccinatoria)*, a vigorous evergreen climber in temperate regions.

CHAPTER THREE

Back and Side Yards

relaxation and recreation

My garden paths that turn and wind
And lead me far from daily grind
Of tasks not wholly to my mind
Are paths of peace.

—Edith Parker Kimball

Far right, a patio situated on the west side of the house was far too hot until the owners added pergolas that mitigate the effects of the sun. These charming structures obscure any views down into the garden area while also providing architectural interest.

Front yards certainly provide new ground in the search for privacy, but it is the backyard that is and always has been the main outdoor destination and private domain for most homes. Depending on your property, the side yard—an often-neglected or even forgotten space—may also be incorporated into the overall landscape scheme as yet another locale for a secluded garden spot.

There are a number of features that will make up your ideal outdoor residential environment, ranging from places for repose and relaxation to a cookout area and nook for alfresco dining, and from specific recreational facilities to plots for special gardens. To understand how privacy can be designed into your landscape, let us begin by analyzing some of these elements and exploring examples of how others have resolved similar challenges.

Patios and Terraces

*I*f you are building a new home or remodeling an existing one, you have some control over the placement of patios and terraces. In densely populated areas where visual privacy is difficult to achieve, putting a patio on a particular side of the house can mean the difference between having a secluded space and one that is open to the view of nearby residences. This is why it is important to survey your environs to determine where the exposed areas are and then to analyze how these spaces can be privatized.

Most of us are not the original builders of our homes but rather the second or third—or even later—owners of our residences, and must deal with existing conditions and configurations. But, as we explored in the preceding chapter, even though a terrace or patio may not be in the area we would have chosen because of excessive noise from neighbors or traffic or because a higher building looms over it, we can take steps to buffer intrusive sounds and shield portions of the space from view.

A friend faced a similar problem in the rear yard of the home he purchased in Los Angeles. The lot is sandwiched between three-story homes. As luck would have it, he is a landscape architect. Unlike the previous owners, who had apparently found the problem of obtaining privacy in the yard too daunting and never planted so much as a shade tree, he quickly recognized the possibilities for sheltering the yard from curious gazes and doing so without blocking the sun or shutting out the light.

After laying a patio, he erected a two-story deck attached to the house. While the upper portion is exposed to view—although this was subsequently ameliorated somewhat by large potted plants—the lower portion is open so that the floor of the deck above becomes a roof over a portion of the patio below. This secluded retreat is adjacent to the master bedroom and provides a cozy spot for enjoying the garden without venturing out into it.

Next came the greenery. As a Cuban expatriate, he chose a plant palette that was tropical, including many genera which, with a bit of extra irrigation, would prosper in the benign southern California climate. To block views into the yard and to filter some of the traffic noise and smog, around the perimeter he planted giant

At right, a virtual jungle in the heart of the city was planted and nurtured by the homeowner in a quest for privacy. The sweeping fronds and dense plantings camouflage the yard. The same goal motivated the family whose tract home was too near its neighbors, far right. Coast redwoods *(Sequoia sempervirens)* and other evergreens now shield their patio after just two seasons.

64

timber bamboo *(Phyllostachys bambusoides)*, which soars to 45 feet (13.5m) or more; *Tupidanthus calyptratus*, which closely resembles the popular house plant umbrella tree *(Schefflera actinophylla)*, producing similar tiers of long-stalked leaves that radiate outward to mimic an open umbrella, and reach 20 feet (6m); weeping Chinese banyan *(Ficus benjamina)*, another universal indoor tree, which attains more than 35 feet (10.5m) of height and whose drooping branches are thickly covered with bright green oval leaves; and giant bird of paradise *(Strelitzia nicolai)*, which forms clumps of stalks topped by banana tree–like leaves and reaches 30 feet (9m).

Understory plants include many species of palms, climbers such as paper flower *(Bougainvillea* sp.), and tropical blooming shrubs and perennials, including ginger and Kaffir lily *(Clivia miniata)*.

From without, the effect is of an overgrown jungle created by the evergreen branches and fronds that arch over the patio. From within, the perception is that one is in a stunning private Eden of tropical splendor.

Smaller patios and terraces may not need such extensive greenscaping to shield them. Often, all that is required is a hedgerow or screen of

dense foliage trees placed at exposed points. In mild-winter climates, where outdoor spaces are often used year-round, evergreen species, such as Indian laurel fig *(Ficus macrocarpa nitida)*, yew pine *(Podocarpus macrophyllus)*, and brush cherry *(Syzygium paniculatum)*, make effective screens. In areas where winter brings freezes, try either deciduous trees or evergreen hedges of box *(Buxus* sp.) or yew *(Taxus* sp.) to establish your backyard patio screening.

Many city patios and terraces that we have seen have two problems that preclude the planting of hedges and screening trees: either they are completely paved over or they are too small to accommodate the width of most hedge shrubs and trees. Nevertheless, enterprising city dwellers who yearn for a sheltering green canopy can resolve these dilemmas. One of the most successful, tried-and-true solutions is to erect

enclosures of lattice screening or trellising on which are trained evergreen or deciduous vines. For spaces exposed from above, a roof of the same material may be constructed so that climbing plants may be coaxed over it.

An option that many patio and terrace gardeners choose is to encircle the patio with pots or planters, of which there are so many wonderful styles. Fill them with evergreen material that can be sheared or espaliered to control its width to create living walls. Some of the species perfect for this application are English holly *(Ilex aquifolium)*, evergreen euonymus *(Euonymus japonica)*, Grecian laurel *(Laurus nobilis)*, myrtle *(Myrtus communis)*, and sweet olive *(Osmanthus fragrans)*, although there are many additional choices available in mild-winter climates.

An urban gardener we know who lives in a town house designed her small terrace for maximum privacy and personality by surrounding it with a row of simple potted evergreens. She then painted each pot a different Crayola hue. With the addition of a 1950s-style garden table and chair set, each element painted in its own primary color, she achieved a private and personality-filled spot for enjoying the outdoors despite her location amid big-city towers.

The waterfront deck at right needs little screening—indeed, the unobstructed view outward is a chief source of pleasure for this family. For those relaxing in the deck chairs, the vertical and horizontal elements of the railing provide a touch of privacy. If a denser screen was wanted, the railing would be an ideal framework on which to train climbing plants.

Decks and Porches

*M*ost of the techniques described above will work equally well for exposed decks and porches. It is as easy to retrofit them with sight barriers as it is to screen patios—perhaps easier, since there are secure vertical and horizontal elements in place to which one can attach trellis and lattice panels. Often, only those sections of a deck or porch that are open to public view, or where unattractive views beyond one's property are visible, need screening. For decks and porches that are very exposed or extremely close to neighbors' homes, try installing tightly woven lattice or custom trellises stained or otherwise finished to blend with the rest of the structure. Even without a mantle of climbing greenery, these screens are attractive and effective shields against visual intrusions, yet never create a closed-in feeling.

Mature trees and a
high wall protect
the backyard patio,
left, from view.

Cookout and Dining Areas

*H*aving secreted your garden away from the intrusions of noise, neighbors, and other distractions, you may discover a wish to create special-use garden "rooms" for pursuing certain activities apart from the rest of the garden. Cooking and outdoor dining are among the greatest of garden pleasures—and designing a distinctive environment for their enjoyment is fairly simple.

In a large yard, a separate structure with a screening roof, such as a pergola, arbor, or pavilion with a lattice or batten overhead or a solid roof, will provide, in addition to privacy, shelter from the elements. One family solved the problem nicely by combining an outdoor kitchen and alfresco dining space inside a spacious gazebo—which also added architectural interest to their otherwise prairie-flat garden.

Another family discovered, after an initial cookout misadventure in their newly remodeled yard, that they needed not just screening from overlooking houses on both sides, but some method of discouraging uninvited party-crashing yellow jackets. These carnivorous wasps are drawn to

both the aroma of barbecues and the presence of sugar and are apparently emboldened by the sight of cowering humans.

This family found their haven in a detached, screened summer room

that gives them a sequestered retreat for outdoor cooking and dining, protected against interloping insects.

Overheads and Coverings

*S*ome form of roofing is often needed over garden rooms where family and guests gather—for both screening and protection from sun and weather. There are benefits to roofing a variety of garden areas, including dining facilities, spas, bathhouses, potting areas, and, perhaps, secret gardens and retreats.

You have many more options for roof coverings than you might imagine. The one that is finally chosen should provide the shelter needed to protect the space below from excessive rain and sunlight as well as provide the level of privacy desired.

Laths and battens Pressure-treated or naturally rot-resistant laths and battens, as well as two-by-two and two-by-four dimensional lumber, are most commonly used to cover arbors, pergolas, and loggias. They can be spaced on rafters to admit the precise amount of light desired or create the ideal level of brightness for shade-preferring plants. The interplay of patterns created by the light shining through strips of wood and plant material will add another layer of visual interest to your space. If, however, total protection from the weather is wanted, the roof should be solid, and this can be accomplished with traditional roofing methods and materials.

Bamboo and woven reeds Rolls of these two natural materials are relatively inexpensive and will survive the rigors of harsh weather for at least a few seasons before replacement is needed. When rolled over and anchored against the wind to rafters, they block most of the light. They

can be installed to roll back and forth to adjust the amount of light that reaches the floor below. Perfect for gardens with an Eastern feel, they work equally well in less formal garden designs, imparting a simple, natural sense of shelter.

Canvas An incredibly versatile material that is growing in popularity as a cover for outdoor rooms, brightly

colored or natural canvas effectively provides both privacy and a sunscreen. It can be draped overhead or used to curtain off an area where you wish to create a truly private niche. Vinyl-coated canvas is considerably more weather-resistant. Note that because of the tightness of its weave, heat may build up under canvas on torrid days.

Vinyl sheeting/Lexan Vinyl-based materials in flat and corrugated profiles are available and offer protection for people, outdoor furniture, and accessories when affixed to overhead rafters. Although available in colors, the most unobtrusive are the untinted translucent and smoked opaque types. Lexan is less affected by UV rays and clear Lexan is virtual-

ly invisible. Like other sheet goods, these should be attached to overheads with rustproof galvanized or zinc-coated screws or other fasteners.

Shade cloth One of the most versatile of all materials for roofing structures is a shade cloth made of woven nylon or vinyl. There are lightweight and heavy-duty cloths available in a variety of weaves with the ability to block from 10 to 80 percent of the sun's rays. While shade cloths provide privacy and shelter from the sun, they afford only minimal protection from the rain. The most attractive way to utilize shade cloth is to stretch it tightly over the rafters and staple it in place. To prevent sags, batten supports may be needed.

A shaded area in the garden is often a desirable and elusive goal, particularly if there is a shortage of mature trees. One solution, shown in two examples at left, and above, is to install an overhead covering that will not only provide shelter but will also help create a pleasant outdoor room.

Screening Storage and Utility Facilities

Storage and utility structures can be landscape assets, too. At right, an attractive niche provides a hidden bicycle storage area. Below, a handsome boat and garden equipment storage shed echoes the style of the adjoining house.

*W*ithout question, the most attractive storage buildings are those designed to blend architecturally with the style of the residence, but this is seldom the case when one purchases an existing home with outbuildings. While these structures may be sound and well constructed, they are seldom visually appealing.

It is often desirable to shield from view these storage and potting sheds and other necessary structures for containing the clutter of tools and

equipment required to maintain the garden, as well as sites where composting is done. Soil amendments, pots, and kindred paraphernalia always need screening. This can usually be done with a shrub or two or a hedgerow, but you may also wish to consider carefully placed fencing, screens, and trellises, which work equally well for blocking from view the sometimes unavoidable clutter.

If there are existing or planned outbuildings in the garden, the logical place for locating utility areas is behind them, space permitting. This enables one to attach trellises and roofs to the walls of the outbuilding

to create a screened and sheltered location for stashing newly purchased stock until it can be planted, for setting up compost bins, and for storing extra paving and other materials destined for future use.

In most cases, all that is needed to quickly fashion a screen around unsightly work or storage areas is to install lattice panels of the appropriate size. Fencing panels offer an equally easy solution. If desired, vines may be grown on these screens to add a softening touch and a bit of color.

Below is a combination garden storage and potting shed with trellises on which vining plants are trained, lending the little shed an English country air.

Backyard Fences and Walls

The ideal fence provides privacy, yet allows the passage of breezes and some light. Below, greenstuff relieves the plain facade of a sturdy, full-height fence. Far right is a wall that has been color-coated to blend with the residence it protects. Native plants help soften the impact of its mass.

Fences cost far less to build than walls and provide immediate privacy and security. Hedges are considered to be friendlier, but require several seasons to mature. Also, if one of the shrubs in a hedge dies, it creates a breach that is difficult to fill with a replacement shrub of the same size. Still, there is nothing in the garden more pleasing to the eye than the symmetry and elegance of a healthy, neatly shorn hedge of box running across the landscape.

In many sections of North America, and even some urban areas abroad, developers of residential communities are required by law or historical precedent to install fencing between lots to mark property lines. Usually, these are merely utilitarian structures devoid of finish or charm. They provide precious little privacy and serve only as a demarcation line between houses and as devices to confine (or block access to) children and pets.

If you are in this situation, which is often the case when a previously owned home is purchased, there are several options to help beautify and privatize. One solution can be what one California landscape architect does for his clients as part of an overall landscape plan—erecting a lattice fence against the developer-built fence or wall and training climbing plants on it so that, in time, it obscures the homely common barrier with greenery.

A second solution is to replace an existing common fence with something more to one's liking. This, of course, means discussing the proposal with the neighbors sharing the fence and reaching an accord on the style and design. In this case, the neighbors should not be expected to share the cost of the new barrier, even though they will benefit from it as before, since they did not initiate the

MAINTAINING "GOOD NEIGHBOR" RELATIONSHIPS

While there may be some truth in the aphorism that high fences make good neighbors, the fence itself can create ill will on the part of the neighbor(s) who must share it. Erecting a tall fence may alter a desirable view from the neighbor's yard or create a shady area that kills part of his or her lawn.

Hedges and tall trees, to a lesser extent, create similar problems, and those that have two or three seasons of litter (spent blooms, seedpods, haws, leaves) are especially invasive to some homeowners who may feel more than a bit set upon by these botanical interlopers.

It is a fact of life, truer today than ever before, that one cannot please everyone. It is the diversity of choice and taste that makes a society interesting. Your preference for a particular fence style or plant palette may not be what your neighbors would choose. But when plantings and barriers are common—shared by homeowners on or near the property line—some effort ought to be made to preserve the goodwill that neighbors should feel toward one another. Often, the courtesy of discussing with one's neighbors proposed plans for a fence or planting is sufficient to avoid the genesis of hard feelings that can escalate into a Hatfield and McCoy– like feud and polarize a neighborhood.

replacement of what was to them apparently a perfectly satisfactory fence.

Sometimes, all that may be needed to transform a deteriorated common fence into a handsome structure is to rehabilitate it with needed repairs and give it a finish that complements the trim or color of one's house. Additionally, the surface may be softened by planting upright shrubs against it or, as mentioned earlier, festooning it with vining material.

Even the humble chain-link fence, that homeliest (and probably most frequently used) of all structural barriers, can be enhanced by electrostatic painting in an unobtrusive color, such as forest green. It can then be further camouflaged with evergreen climbers, such as five-leaf akebia *(Akebia quinata)*, jasmines, and honeysuckles.

Side Yards

$\mathcal{S}$ ide yards are sometimes given only passing interest and attention by designers and homeowners because of their narrowness, visibility to neighbors and passersby, or exposure. The result is that side yards are usually the "orphans" of the landscape, ending up as mere transition areas to get from one part of the yard to another. Often, the side yard lies between houses and is so sheltered that no attempt is made to establish a garden of any consequence in it.

In the hands of a competent and imaginative designer, a side yard can be an asset, a destination in the garden, rather than a traverse point to somewhere else. If it is exposed to view from the street or neighbors' windows face it, screens and plantings can, as shown earlier, solve this lack of privacy. We have seen the narrowest of side yards overlooked by neighbors reclaimed for family use simply by installing at the property line tall lattice screens on which climbers are trained. If no adjacent homes overlook the space, the obvious solution is to plant an informal hedge or erect a fence or wall of the appropriate height.

A shady side yard provides an opportunity to establish a garden of shade-preference and shade-tolerant plants—a wonderful, moist microclimate where one can sling a hammock on a sultry afternoon.

Often, homeowners are stymied when considering what will grow in medium to deep shade. Their first inclination may be to attempt a lawn, but although some fescue blends tolerate a bit of shade, other turf grass won't perform well without four or five hours of daily sun. There are, however, several handsome groundcovers that prosper in shady situations around stepping stones and other hardscape and under tree canopies. Among these are allegheny spurge (*Pachysandra procumbens*), bugleweed (*Ajuga* sp.), English ivy (*Hedera helix* hybrids), Kew wintercreeper (*Euonymus fortunei* 'Kewensis'), and partridge berry (*Michelia repens*).

Perennials that prefer a shady nook include bear's breech (*Acanthus mollis*), cardinal flower (*Lobelia cardinalis*), forget-me-not (*Myosotis scorpioides*), ligularia (*Ligularia dentata*), lily turf (*Liriope* sp.), plantain lily (*Hosta* hybrids), primrose (*Primula* sp.), Virginia bluebells (*Mertensia virginica*), and wake robin (*Trillium* sp.).

Some of the longer-lived flowering annuals that are ideal for moist shade are begonia (*Begonia* × *semperflorens-cultorum*), campanula (*Campanula* sp.), flossflower (*Ageratum houstonianum*), flowering tobacco (*Nicotiana alata*), forget-me-not (*Myosotis sylvatica*), and sweet violet (*Viola odorata*).

Most side yards are effectively ignored by homeowners, who are often stymied about what to do with the usually shady, seldom-used space. Here, a bedroom door opens onto a small, secluded retreat. Shade-loving plants, interlock flooring, and a non-linear bed give this previously dull spot appeal.

Left: Who says a parking area has to be ugly? These homeowners established an attractive parking area for guests, enclosed by a pair of decorative gates.

Containers and Porch and Window Boxes

Work areas exposed to view, such as this potting and propagation room, may be dressed up with splashes of color and pots of greenery. Such spaces are ideal for displaying collections of vintage garden tools, birdhouses, and the like.

Plantings in containers are both pretty and practical in the home landscape. They enable one to bring traditional garden plants and seasonals, like bulbs and wildflowers, near the house for close-up appreciation.

Kitchen gardens just outside the door are immediately accessible in collections of pots and boxes. Herbs are easily harvested and a few leaves of lettuce or a tomato ripened to perfection may be plucked without trudging into the garden—if, indeed, one has a garden.

Contained shrubs and trees are also ideal living screens that may be trundled about to provide service where they are needed, or merely situated where they give visual pleasure. We have maintained orchards of dwarf fruit trees in tubs for a number of years. They give yeoman's service as colorful spring accents when in bloom, and sources of delectable, pesticide-free treats and decorative screens blocking neighbors' views into our patio through the summer.

Window boxes are decorative old-world embellishments that add to the charm of villages and towns throughout Europe. Their popularity has waxed and waned in the United States, where they are currently enjoying a renaissance.

Minigardens on sills or suspended just below windows bring color and aroma close enough to be enjoyed from inside one's home. They provide gardening possibilities for gardenless city highrise dwellers and enhance the appearance of many residential exteriors when box designs are matched with architectural style.

Most plants grown in them require regular pinching, pruning, and plucking, and some need seasonal replacement for boxes to be decorative assets instead of eyesores.

Techniques and Maintenance

*S*uccess with contained gardens begins with using pots, tubs, and boxes with drainage holes of adequate size and number to allow excess water to run out so that plant roots are not drowned. Additional holes can easily be added to most containers with a drill bit made of the proper material and a power drill: spade bit for plastic and wood; masonry types for stone, concrete, and brick; and high-speed tungsten steel for lead and other metals.

Potting media for containers should be comparable to that often recommended ideal, "good garden loam." This is generally defined as soil that is composed of silt, sand, clay particles, and some humus. To duplicate this as closely as possible, a number of organic amendments are blended to create a synthetic soil. The ingredients are sharp sand, milled peat, well-rotted (composted) steer manure, composted redwood or fir bark, perlite or vermiculite, and poultry litter. The result is a friable,

Ornamental pots of mixed plantings are useful accents for high-profile areas that need a splash of color. Above, a ledge of annuals and perennials dresses up this window, providing visual interest from within and without. Below, containers of colorful plants placed in front of floor-to-ceiling windows allow the people indoors to enjoy the garden sights.

79

Where there is no open ground in which to grow a floral garden, containers and window boxes are effective options, enabling one to bring the beauty and aroma of flowers close to the house.

fertile mix that holds some moisture, yet drains well, and is nutrient-rich. When acid-loving plants are grown, the proportion of peat moss in relation to the other ingredients is increased two-or threefold.

Many contained gardens fail from neglect and the most common oversight is failure to irrigate regularly. Unlike plant roots in a traditional plot, roots in containers can't roam far in their quest for moisture. Without periodic rainfall, water must be provided twice a week (minimally) either by hand or automatically through a drip irrigation system.

Fertilizing is not important in the culture of healthy plants, provided they are planted in humus-rich media. If additional nutrients are needed, such as foods for acid-prefer-ence plants like azalea, rhododen-dron, gardenia, and blueberries, this can be supplied by working a high-nitrogen organic fertilizer into the topsoil and watering it in. Varieties that prefer a neutral growing medium will benefit from a topdressing of composted manure in spring and fall.

Regular pruning, pinching, and grooming will keep contained plant-ings vigorous and attractive. Leggy vines always benefit from heading back, and taking out the growing tips of many plants (exclusive of most conifers) will force growth back into foliage below the cuts and nips, resulting in a bushier specimen. Dead and dying plants should be removed at the first sign of decline to make room for healthy companions.

Pests and diseases are just as like-ly to attack contained gardens as they are conventional ones. Roses seem doomed to be victimized by aphids wherever they are grown, and scales are epidemic in some regions on woody plants. Nearly every pest or malady that afflicts ornamental and crop plants can be controlled by or-ganic means—environmentally safe sprays, baits, and beneficial insects. These earth- and user-friendly solu-tions are available at many garden centers and through a number of mail order sources.

Gardening in containers enables those who live in harsh-winter re-gions above USDA Zone 8 to grow a wide variety of frost-tender species, from agapanthus to zantedeschia and from citrus to bougainvillea. In in-hospitable climates, these tender species can be spirited indoors or to a greenhouse at the first hint of frost, then returned to their allocated spot with the first breath of spring.

Gallery of Fences and Walls

Barrier and enclosure structures are as varied in their design and color as the gardens they surround. Barricades are as old as mankind, but we have come a long way since the first fences of thorny branches and walls of stone rubble were constructed by early humans to protect themselves from predatory beasts and rival clans.

Following is a gallery of popular fence and wall styles for residential properties. There are low fences and walls whose task is merely to define boundaries and contain pets and children, as well as tall, solid, imposing forms for privacy and security.

Combining the benefits of privacy and security, these barriers are also handsome complements to the landscape. Left, the scalloped treatment of the pickets is more pleasing to the eye than if they had been set on an even plane. Below, a stunning wall was designed with mosaic preciseness for visual interest.

A host of decorative and functional fences and walls is shown on these two pages, illustrating some of the principles outlined in the text. Above left, an attractive modified picket style fence on a brick footing; above right, a mortared fieldstone wall; right, a fence with lattice panels that provide an efficient framework for anchoring climbing plants.

Left, a beautifully-designed and constructed curved brick entry-wall; below left, a durable wrought iron picket fence; below right, a glass block wall, a non-traditional fencing material that is growing in popularity because it completely blocks views into the garden, but does not shut out light.

CHAPTER FOUR

Garden Getaways

Whoever has a garden has a perennial
source of interest, whether the garden
itself be large or small.

—Helen Ashe Hays

On the opposite page is a gazebo with all the comforts of home—a complete cook-out center, refrigerator, and ample dining space. In regions where insects are a problem, gazebos can easily be screened.

Over the last decade, gardens have become much more than merely the land that surrounds the house. We have watched as that previously de rigueur feature of all front yards, the rolling swath of impeccable lawn, has given way to more imaginative approaches, from simply adding island beds of, say, roses and perennials to the more dramatic transformation entailed in paving over and walling in the lawn to serve as a courtyard floor.

There are also massive changes being wrought in the backyard, which was once the children's domain—a place for them to romp out of harm's way. As families are discovering that they want to spend more leisure time at home enjoying their immediate environs, communing with nature, entertaining friends, and puttering in a garden of one sort or another, it has become increasingly important to design the backyard to accommodate these needs.

What has actually happened is that many of us have come full circle and returned to the home-based comforts and entertainments of a bygone era—a time when families played croquet and whiffleball in their yards and grew their own ingredients for sachets and potpourri—when the garden represented a whole world of family experience.

Hanna Rion, an Ulster County, New York, gardener and author, defined this spirit in *Let's Make a Flower Garden* (1912): "When you buy a piece of land, remember—you own all above it; you own that far reach of ether in which the stars drift over your land, the moon as it hangs above your trees, the sun as it passes through your sky—and best of all you possess all the dreams which lie between you and infinity."

A growing number of families are finding contentment in the diversions available in their own backyards. As they reimagine these spaces and enhance their outdoor facilities to provide settings for a range of activities, a wealth of exciting design possibilities are emerging. Likewise, as people spend more time out in their yards, strategies for achieving privacy—both for the garden itself and for those within the garden— become very creative.

Gazebos and Pavilions

Open-air garden rooms are in vogue among garden designers today, although we should probably say *still* in vogue, since these niceties can be traced back to ancient Egypt and China. They were used by pharaohs, emperors, and members of the privileged classes for much the same purpose as we utilize them today—to enjoy their gardens in comfort. Architects in ancient China, Greece, and Italy designed porticoes for their wealthy patrons so that they could take pleasure from garden vistas protected from the often oppressive heat of the summer sun and from the occasional downpour.

In nineteenth-century England, the garden-loving Victorians defined and refined gazebos, adorning these roofed, open-on-all-sides structures with intricate and fanciful fretwork and elevating them in importance to frequently used outdoor retreats for teas, trysts, and tranquil escapes. Across the Atlantic, Americans soon became enamored of and adopted the gazebo for their own gardens. By the turn of the century, it had become the most popular of all garden structures. Although the popularity of

usually require some provision for protecting garden users from the power of the sun's rays—a roof of lattice or lumber laid on edge, a canopy of canvas, or some other cover that blocks, filters, or regulates sunlight.

In rooms where furniture, appliances, and other amenities are kept, a solid, protective overhead is necessary. For a pleasing and private way to achieve cover without claustrophobia, try installing open latticework as walls and training vines or espaliered shrubs or trees on them.

Siting of the open-air room must be well thought out to maximize the usefulness and comfort of the space. For optimum shade and coolest temperatures, a gazebo, deck, or patio should be placed in a north-facing position. An eastern exposure is slightly less shady, since it receives morning sunlight only. South-facing sites are usually bright and sunny all day, with a

At far left, a redwood gazebo provides a sheltered vantage point from which to experience this serene, natural garden. Left, in more arid regions, where rain is infrequent, a lattice overhead is all that is necessary for protection. The oriental influence is obvious in this serene design.

gazebos waned somewhat after World War II, recently they have once again found favor, giving rise to a new generation of designers and builders.

Contemporary outdoor shelters are designed to achieve the same goals our ancient ancestors had and would turn the average Roman of Caesar's time green with envy. Modern building materials, screening, and canopy options make it possible to design a garden room that is truly weather-tight, not to mention free of the hordes of flying pests that doubtlessly plagued our historical predecessors' outdoor festivities.

Since most garden rooms are used primarily in warm weather, they

west-facing location being the hottest, receiving the most intense afternoon sunlight.

Train vines and climbers to clamber up the pillars of a gazebo, or place containers filled with bright blooms around the perimeter of the structure to truly blur the distinction between garden and structure. If you wish to block views into the gazebo, thick trails of ivy can form a green curtain. Layers of vegetation will lend the composition a touch of gothic mystery, a sense that nature is reclaiming the land. Canvas blinds can be tucked under the inner eaves to be rolled down in the event that full privacy is wanted.

Whatever the style of your particular structure, a gazebo in a corner of the garden is an irresistible lure—a romantic destination, shelter from a sudden summer deluge, a magical place to sequester oneself with a book, a craft, or an easel. A gazebo also offers the possibility of a private moment even in a garden filled with family members pursuing various activities—and sometimes, a brief respite, a momentary haven from the hubbub, is all that is needed.

Equally popular today are the modern interpretations of the classic pavilion, a flat-roofed open-air room. More practical than traditional gazebos, and sometimes called cabanas,

these versatile spaces may house, in addition to chaises and other furniture, outdoor kitchens, dining facilities, changing rooms for a pool, and even storage closets for garden equipment or pool maintenance. A pavilion may be located closer to the house, next to a pool, or at the far end of the garden, depending on how it will be used. Pavilion architecture is very adaptable as well, lending itself to styles from Bauhaus to Zen. To soften the harder lines of pavilion or cabana architecture and to provide a leafy, privacy-enhancing screen, try training vines to drape across the roof and supporting walls or pillars or add strategically placed potted evergreens.

The floating gazebo (far left) among the trees in director-comedian David Steinberg's California back yard is set amid lush vegetation, making it seem even more secluded. Above, a sumptuous poolside gazebo for stylish family cookouts.

Arbors

*L*ike gazebos, arbors—shelters created by branches, vines, or lattice—were once found in nearly every North American and British backyard. Some were commodious and innovative in design, others only large enough for a couple to repose under a froth of gingerbread fretwork. Recently experiencing a renaissance, arbors are reappearing in backyards as gardeners seek to add accents both useful and attractive to their landscapes.

From a design standpoint, the arbor offers an essential element of vertical interest, lifting the eye and extending the garden upward. An arbor can literally transform a landscape, taking it from flat and boring to distinctive and exciting. An arbor may also serve as an entrance from one area of the garden into another—you may wish to separate a children's play space, for example, or a cutting garden, from the rest of the garden. In addition, the arbor actually increases the garden space, allowing plant material to grow upward. Some plants that might do poorly when grown at ground level will thrive with the extra sunlight they receive up above.

Stylized arbors, right, make excellent screens, while also providing anchors for climbing plants and adding vertical interest in the garden.

On a less practical note, an arbor introduces a new, privacy-encouraging mood into the garden. It offers a romantic, secluded spot perfect for a quiet interlude—with a book, a loved one, or just a moment of peace. Shaded and still, the arbor also creates a welcoming and sheltered vantage point from which to look out at the rest of the garden. Screen it with clinging vines or drape it with wisteria, and you have a ready-made, sensually satisfying private garden room.

Again like gazebos, arbor styles vary from ornately Victorian to rustic to starkly modern. The style you select will define the tone of that area of the garden. A white-painted lattice arch covered in fragrant rose blossoms imparts an English-garden feeling to an otherwise typical suburban yard, while an arbor constructed of weathered barn boards and bedecked with grapevines adds a country flavor. For a clean yet interesting look, consider training a variegated ivy (carefully controlled) over a plain metal archway.

Even the smallest of urban backyards can accommodate an arbor tucked into a niche. Many gardening catalogs offer arbors in various shapes and sizes. Add a small bench and you have created a private nook that will soon draw in anyone searching for a moment of private contemplation or the special pleasure of finding quiet repose amid more active garden pursuits.

A corner of this backyard has been transformed into an irresistible retreat spanned by a handmade arbor made for the owner from her own design.

Secret Gardens

Garden hideaways provide secluded, romatic destinations for adults to escape the stresses of the day and demands on their time. These personal sanctuaries can contain many pleasant offerings—a hammock suspended among the trees, a firepit surrounded by cushions or benches for a private marshmallow roast, or a spa tucked away in a remote corner where you can relax and absorb the sensual pleasures of water, color, and scent.

Paramount in importance for a secret garden is that its location be isolated from the mainstream of activity. It should be a place where nothing intrudes, especially prying eyes and noise and other infringements from extraneous sources. A lattice wall, a fence, or even a length of canvas artfully suspended from a metal framework will cloister your retreat visually.

To some extent, well-placed planting can mitigate the clamor of traffic or stereos and television sets blaring through neighborhood windows. How effective these botanical buffers are depends on the closeness of the source of the cacophony and the density of the planting intended to muffle it. The most effective sound dampeners are planted between the source and the private yard in two or more layers. For example, the first planting at the property boundary might be densely leaved evergreen trees, such as cedars (*Cedrus* sp.) and spruces (*Picea* sp.). The second planting, adjacent to the trees, would be a thick hedgerow of evergreen shrubs, such as box (*Buxus sempervirens*) or yew (*Taxus* sp.) in northern climes, and fern pine (*Podocarpus* sp.) or Japanese cleyera (*Cleyera japonica*) in the southern zones. Finally, a trellis wall that is covered with a climber might provide the final bulwark against auditory assaults.

(There is a burgeoning source of noise that no amount of landscaping can modulate and that is the sonic boom–like cannonade of the new generation of auto stereos whose thundering bass can penetrate armor plate. The only hope for relief from this mobile fusillade is the enactment of a local noise abatement ordinance.)

Dense plantings are also somewhat effective in filtering pollution, dust, cooking odors, and other airborne contaminants. It is necessary only to determine the direction of the prevailing winds and then install greenscaping to intercept them.

Once these practical plantings have been introduced, it is time to consider adding the sensory stimuli—aromatic plants like jasmine and scented roses that perfume the air and colorful blooms that provide a feast for the eyes. If the retreat will be visited in the evening, a white garden may create a lovely enclosure for a private moonlit moment.

As we have noted, water is an evocative element in the garden, even when it is not seen, but only heard. When the source is hidden, people are often drawn to it, consumed by a desire to trace it to its origin. In a secret garden, a fountain provides the background music for relaxation, deepening the visitor's sense of having found a secluded Eden far from the public world. A pool invites you to dangle your toes in its cooling depths on a sultry day. After dark, moving water can be lit to provide a fascinating ballet of iridescent droplets dancing in air.

Carefully chosen plant material and a well-planned design can help create secret gardens such as the one at left, which is hidden from view, yet is only 15 feet (4.5m) from a busy street. Far left, a secret sanctuary features a garden statue set amid the blooms.

Night Gardens

*M*any people, particularly those whose careers keep them away from home until after nightfall, find that with a source of light in the garden (beyond what the moon and stars, charming though they are, can offer), they are drawn outdoors long after sunset. Once night has fallen, the garden takes on a different aura in the soft glow of artificial light, creating a mood that is both restful and romantic. Water features and sculpture come alive at night when illuminated by a spot adjusted to a soft focus setting. Nightlighting is the key to extending the length of time you can enjoy the garden.

Illuminating the garden, pathways, and perimeter of your home has obvious benefits even for families who do not spend a lot of time in the garden at night. It makes the yard safer after dark, especially for guests, by revealing steps, level changes, and obstructions that could cause mishaps. A well-lit exterior deters intruders and makes family members feel secure. Finally, an aesthetically pleasing lighting scheme adds a whole new dimension to the beauty of house and garden.

A well-lit garden need not sacrifice privacy. In the last decade, great strides have been made in the techniques of outdoor lighting. No longer is it your only option to employ floodlight fixtures that are more suitable for illuminating a penal compound. The new generation of outdoor lights are subtle, yet efficient low-voltage fixtures that are available in a number of configurations, from walk lights to focusable spots that can be hidden in trees and under eaves.

In addition to being just as effective as standard wattage fixtures in lighting walks and other areas in yard and garden, low-voltage systems are easy to install without the need for trenching for conduit. Since the fixtures operate on a mere 12 volts, there is no danger of a lethal shock if the power line is accidentally severed with a shovel. To hide the wires from sight, simply cover them with mulch.

Outdoor lighting specialists are available in most cities of moderate size, but there is no reason why a

The garden at night can be a magical place, as seen in the photographs on these two pages.

homeowner cannot design and install an effective nightlighting system. There are kits available that contain an assortment of fixtures (from mushroom walklights to spotlights that can be focused), as well as ample electrical cable and a step-down transformer-controller that reduces 110-volt household current to a safe 12 volts.

Spotlights create wonderful nighttime illumination when used to highlight a tree or tall planting by aiming them up into the branches, where the play of light and dark lends drama to the canopy of foliage above. Create what is called a "moonlight" effect by hiding spotlights in the crown of the tree and pointing them downward to make pools of light. Or point a spot so that it shines through foliage, casting a dramatic leafy shadow pattern. Spotlights are also effective when used as "wall sweeps" along the foundation. This technique lights up the facade and silhouettes shrubs and trees that lie against it.

Point downlights at strategic spots along paths, walks, and steps to shed light for those moving about in the garden after dark. These fixtures are the only ones that should be visible; the others should be secreted behind shrubs or structural elements so only the effect is seen, not the source. Small, twinkling bulbs are an exception to this rule: string them under stair treads or around the lip of spas to shed enough light for safety but not so much brightness as to be intrusive. The ubiquitous novelty bulbs (shaped like cows, peppers, and what-have-you) may be best left for providing decoration at theme parties.

For convenience and safety, most low-voltage outdoor systems are equipped with a transformer that has a built-in timer control that operates either by programming it to turn the lights on for a set number of hours or by a sensor that turns the lights on at dusk and off at dawn. An additional benefit of low-voltage lighting is that it can be operated for only pennies a night.

Many homeowners combine the two, using low voltage for accent lighting in the garden and 110-voltage for task lighting in such things as outdoor kitchens, potting areas, and other spaces where brighter illumination is desired.

Vegetable gardens are often screened from view because of periods of barrenness and occasional gaps between crop plants. Here a diagonal-lattice screen is used to hide the vegetable garden—although a "window" above the gate allows for a peek inside.

Specialty Gardens

Gardens planned for specific plant types need not be extensive to be functional. You can tuck an herb or kitchen garden in a sunny corner near the house, or a cutting garden may be established in an out-of-the-way niche that gets good light most of the day.

Raised beds are ideal for these production gardens, when filled with fertile soil amended to nurture the plants grown in them. For example, plants that prefer an acid root run should be grown in a mix that is predominantly peat. You will find that it

is much easier to custom tailor a soil mix to the tastes of specific species in raised beds (and containers) than in a conventional plot where the ground is often compacted and rocky.

Those who prefer a manicured backyard domain and find the occasional barrenness of a cutting, kitchen, or herb garden unappealing need not abandon the idea of a specialty garden. These transitional plots can be hidden behind outbuildings, hedges, lattice screens, or other barriers so that they are not visible from the house.

Cutting gardens are invaluable assets, providing seasonal blooms and materials for floral arrangements

throughout the house. This is a boon to all those who enjoy the beauty of fresh flowers indoors—and especially for those flower lovers who live in an area remote from traditional sources of cut flowers. In addition, a cutting garden enables you to grow a wide range of plants, some of which are not available in most flower shops.

Gardens that are harvested periodically will have gaps between the remaining plants and may look a bit bedraggled. For those in northerly regions, there is also the fallow winter season when the gardens are barren. Many gardeners thus choose to camouflage their functional gardens by erecting a structure in front of them, such as a fence or lattice screen to which vines or climbers cling.

Well-planned cutting gardens are a mix of annuals, biennials, perennials, and bulbs so that there is always something to snip for a quick bouquet and something coming along for tomorrow. For versatility and contrast in floral arrangements, shrubs that yield long-lived flowers, such as lilacs, viburnums, and, of course, roses, are absolutely essential.

Above is another architecturally integrated screen that blends with the house and shields from view a cutting garden.

At left, a beguiling cutting garden that is an irresistible lure with its inviting bench and exhilarating view. Included in this view are candle larkspur *(Delphinium elatum)*, alstroemeria (*Alstroemeria* sp.), sweet alyssum *(Lobulara maritima)*, pansy *(Viola wittrockiana)*, which is also shown at right, in pots placed along a window ledge, and dusty miller *(Senecio cineraria)*. Not shown are a number of roses grown for their captivating scent.

PLANTS FOR CUTTING GARDENS

Following is a list, by no means definitive, of some of the best species for cutting gardens that will provide ample material for arrangements throughout the growing season.

Achillea species, yarrow
Alcea rosea, hollyhock
Alchemilla species, lady's mantle
Anemone × hybrida, Japanese anemone
Antirrhinum majus, snapdragon
Artemisia species, artemisia
Astilbe × arendsii, false spiraea
Calendula officinalis, calendula
Callistephus chinensis, China aster
Campanula species, bellflower (perennials, annuals, biennials)
Centaurea cyanus, bachelor's button
Chaenomeles species, flowering quince
Clarkia amoena, godetia
Consolida ambigua, larkspur
Convallaria majalis, lily of the valley
Coreopsis species, coreopsis
Cosmos bipinnatus, cosmos
Delphinium species, delphinium
Digitalis species, foxglove
Echinacea purpurea, purple coneflower
Echinops exaltatus, globe thistle
Forsythia species, forsythia
Freesia species, freesia
Fritillaria species, fritillaria
Gaillardia × grandiflora, blanketflower
Gerbera jamesonii, Transvaal daisy
Gladiolus species, gladiolus
Gomphrena globosa, globe amaranth
Gypsophila species, baby's-breath
Helianthus annuus, sunflower
Helichrysum bracteatum, strawflower
Heliotropium arborescens, heliotrope
Iris species, iris
Lavandula species, lavender
Liatris spicata, liatris
Lilium species, lily
Limonium perezii, statice
Matthiola incana, stock
Moluccella laevis, bells of Ireland

Narcissus species, miniature and standard daffodils
Paeonia species, peony
Platycodon grandiflorus, balloon flower
Polianthes tuberosa, tuberose
Ranunculus asiaticus, ranunculus
Rosa species, rose
Rudbeckia hirta, gloriosa daisy
Syringa vulgaris, lilac
Tropaeolum majus, nasturtium
Tulipa species, tulip
Verbascum phoeniceum, purple mullein
Veroncia spicata, speedwell
Viburnum species, viburnum
Viola wittrockiana, pansy
Zantedeschia species, calla lily
Zinnia species, zinnia

Kitchen and Herb Gardens

A low fence shields this formal English knot garden—the ultimate refinement of the herb garden, a mainstay of the landscape since medieval times.

In North America, even as late as colonial America, typical plantings around homes were not ornamental, unless incidentally, but were solely devoted to herbs and food crops—the first example on this continent of the edible landscape.

Thereafter, ornamental gardens slowly but surely took over. Vegetable gardens have waxed and waned in popularity since the end of World War II, when fresh produce was once again readily available at the corner market. Nearly every family here and abroad who had an arable plot of land planted a crop garden (called a "victory garden") during the dark years of rationing and privation. After the armistice, many families converted their vegetable gardens into flower beds.

In medieval times, a garden of herbs was not so much an option as a necessity. Herbs were a source of medicines in an age when only a few physicians actively practiced an ersatz form of medicine that was a mixture of alchemy and superstition. Every mother soon became a self-taught herbalist well acquainted with the

virtues of herbs for medicinal and culinary uses. More recently, herb gardens have gained more and more devotees as people begin to discover the usefulness and versatility of these ancient plants.

Today, our motivations for growing produce and herbs are less imperative. With food crops, there is simply no comparison in terms of flavor, aroma, and variety—home-grown far outshines store-bought in every way. Additionally, one can, by adapting organic techniques, ensure that the vegetables and fruit from the home garden are free of harmful pesticide residue.

But one of the most often cited benefits of growing one's own produce is the incredible choice of old-fashioned varieties available that rarely, if ever, are offered in markets.

A popular trend in home gardening is to grow both herb and food crops in raised beds, containers, and planters near the house but screened from view by plantings or other garden elements, such as trellises or decorative fences. This enables one to merely step out the door to harvest what is needed for a meal, giving meaning to the designation "kitchen garden." The only caveat is that these gardens must be sited where they will receive four to six hours of direct sunlight each day for plants to prosper.

A charming example of the kitchen garden is shown here: a mixed planting of vegetables, herbs, and ornamentals in raised beds.

Children's Retreats and Play Areas

Playhouse design is limited only by the imagination (and budget) of the families whose children will claim title. Right, a modest example built for a pre-schooler; below, an extravagant edifice with slides and tower; and, far right, a perfect replica of the owners' house reproduced in miniature.

When children are still young enough to require supervision while at play, their recreation spaces should be in sites where there is an unobstructed view of them from the house while affording as much distance from the street as possible. As children reach school age, they will need and want some privacy. Indeed, they delight in secret hideaways.

For young children, the ultimate escape is a playhouse that can function as a stage for acting and make-believe scenarios, from tea parties to castles. Given a choice, many older children will opt for an arboreal home—a simple platform or a full-blown treehouse—where one can go to daydream, to read, or simply to be alone.

Playhouses can be located just about anywhere there is high visibility space in the garden. One couple with two girls who wanted a playhouse determined that the backyard of their downsized city lot was too small to accommodate anything more than a cutting bed. They retained their architect to design a playhouse that was a replica of their home and placed it in a corner of the front yard. Another family commissioned a two-story playhouse in an unused side yard that was accessible by a bridge leading from the children's bedrooms.

Neither every family nor every yard requires a playhouse in the grand style—and there are plenty of options for more compact and simple playspaces that will satisfy any imaginative child. For the younger set, consider using a low fence to enclose a grassy area that the kids can call their own (away from your precious plantings). A low hedge could also be used as a border to define the children's area. A trellis twined with climbers may serve as a pretty and practical way to separate a playspace from the rest of the backyard without seeming to isolate it. A child's swing set or pool can be placed in a corner of the yard that is fully visible yet defined by a row of miniature evergreens.

With the children's play area an integral part of the backyard garden and at the same time having its own borders, children can be part of the daily life of the garden without feeling that they are underfoot in a grown-up's world.

Down the Garden Path

A footpath or walkway introduces the prospect of a destination in the garden. Even if the path leads the garden stroller just a short distance from the starting point, it nevertheless creates a sense of movement from one area to another. In a small garden, a walkway can make the space seem more commodious; in a more extensive landscape, a path can link smaller garden rooms, creating a sense of intimacy. Walkways may be as rustic as a bark-strewn trail through a natural garden, as formal as a brick footway of intricate design, or anything in between.

In coastal South Carolina, paths are often fashioned from crushed oyster shells which are spread over the native soil. And in Charleston, many an elegant garden is crisscrossed with paths and patios of salvaged material, from broken tiles, shards and—here and there—the odd brick. This crazy-quilt paving technique began to appear early in the city's history, when cobblestones and brick were beyond the financial reach of most residents. Although most homeowners can now afford more extravagant path-

Although often composed of brick, paths in Colonial gardens, such as this fine example in historic Charleston, South Carolina, are equally in character when topped with organic material such as crushed stone, gravel, or—as used here—decomposed granite. Old brick and weathered stone edging keeps the paving material out of beds and gives the pathway an attractive finished look.

ways, the quaint practice of utilizing bits of this and that persists.

There is a wide choice of traditional materials available for making garden paths. These options include brick of various colors; flagstone in an infinite variety of hues; several different types of natural stone, such as granite; precast concrete pavers, from small interlocking units to four-foot-square (372 sq cm) blocks; gravel; decomposed granite (DG); and timber, including tree slices and wood chips.

Some materials are worthy of consideration because of their local availability, which generally means immediate delivery and lower cost. For example, bouquet canyon stone is popular in the western United States, Pennsylvania blue stone in the East.

For the more adventurous garden designer, many nontraditional materials can be pressed into service for a walkway. Stepping stones of distressed metal lend an industrial air to a postmodern garden; concrete arrows could be brightly painted to point to a children's play area.

There are no hard and fast rules about laying in a garden walk, although symmetrical corridors are generally installed in formal settings and meandering, winding paths are

usually found in informal gardens. Walks that disappear around a corner or curve through plantings are intriguing and lure one to explore.

Whatever the style or configuration, consider how your path will be used and whether it should be broad enough to permit two adults to walk comfortably side by side or to accommodate a person maneuvering a wheelbarrow.

Athough a garden path will often lead to a focal point, such as a sundial, fountain, or capriccio, or a destination, such as an arbor or gazebo, it is not necessary to have an end goal. A

charming path may simply wind around a section of the garden, featuring interesting points along the way, leading nowhere.

To lend a walkway an additional source of sensory pleasure, plant an aromatic groundcover between stepping stones that releases its fragrance when trod upon. One of the best of these is creeping thyme (*Thymus serpyllum*).

This formal English-style garden has paths of gravel that intersect at right angles. Gravel drains well and is an ideal surface material, although it is necessary to lay down a weed barrier material before the gravel is spread.

107

CHAPTER FIVE

Setting Scenes

Why keep a garden account
And reckon the cost of pure joy?
Is it not cheap at any price?

—Mabel Osgood Wright

An often overlooked but very effective method of creating privacy lies in giving people something else to look at besides the garden's inhabitants. Indeed, since a major component in the theory of good garden design is how well viewpoints have been established and how effectively the eye is drawn to these tableaux, it sometimes surprises us how infrequently such theories are put into practice.

What elevates a good garden to great status is the designer's awareness of a need for destinations for the eye and how well this objective is achieved. These focal points may be as broad and grand as a panoramic scene framed in the distance or as subtle and focused as a roundel at the end of a pathway. To achieve both privacy and visual interest, the key is to reconfigure those wide, boring expanses of lawn featuring nothing more than the occasional bed into garden rooms that lead the visitor from one place to another, encouraging movement and offering visual rewards to entice wanderers.

Framed as a piece of kinetic art, this view from within of a wall fountain and courtyard garden provides an ever-changing vista through the seasons. Far right, French doors open onto a private patio garden with a number of features to attract the eye.

Enhancing Views from Within

While it may seem obvious, many garden designers overlook one of the most important and appealing views—the view from inside the house looking out into the garden. We have seen scores of stunning gardens that have all the ingredients of good design—balance, unity, proportion, and variety—with no provision made for creating interesting focal points that will please people within the various rooms. Yet these vistas are what engender a sense of peace and spiritual rejuvenation and lure those indoors out for a stroll through the garden.

Too often privacy is achieved by drawn shutters and heavy window coverings that are breached only briefly during the day. A better solution would be to replace these view- and light-blocking coverings with evergreen plantings that accomplish the same purpose but do so without shutting out light, fresh air, and outdoor vistas. "Evergreen" does not mean merely coniferous material, but also the broadleaf genera, which are equally useful in the residential landscape.

Included in the palette should be some aromatic plants for, as Rudyard Kipling aptly noted, "Smells are surer than sounds or sights to make your heart-strings crack." This scented material need not be evergreen and

Containers and window boxes of colorful and aromatic plants can be brought close to the house to establish pretty, sweet-smelling accents just outside windows and doors.

might even be housed in containers so that it can be changed seasonally to provide a fresh viewpoint and a variety of evocative aromas. Among the sweetly fragranced options are jasmine, roses, moonflower, lilac, and lavender, to name a few. There are many more choices available for those who live in mild-winter climates.

Even in winter in areas of seasonal snow, outdoor interest may be created by adding some material that bears a bounty of berries or has colorful or interesting bark. One might also install a feeder outside a window so that native birds will be drawn close in.

If there are French doors that open onto an appropriate space, this might be the ideal site for a personal sanctuary. What better spot for a

melodic fountain in a small outdoor sitting room? Or for a secret garden that fills the living room or bedroom with sweet scents when the doors are flung open in spring and summer?

These verdant retreats provide romantic settings for open-air breakfasts and afternoon teas, for quiet chats with family and friends, or simply to be alone with your thoughts.

Obviously, the first step is to simply look through windows to the garden and analyze views. Is there a specimen tree or shrub that draws the

eye? Where might one be established to create an interesting or colorful accent? Is there a site for an arbor or trellis that would provide visual interest from major windows? If a wall obstructs the view, might installing a fountain or water feature turn a liability into a garden accent? Perhaps a colorful climber could be persuaded to cling to the wall or a fruit tree espaliered to create a focal point where a mere blank fence formerly sat.

ROSES (sweet fragrance)

'Chrysler Imperial'
'Crimson Glory'
'Electron'
'Fragrant Cloud'
'Fragrant Hour'
'Fragrant Memory'
'Mister Lincoln'
'Nymphenburg'

ROSES (old rose fragrance)

'Fashion'
'Gertrude Jekyll'
'Intrigue'
'Mary Rose'
'Penelope'
'Papa Meilland'
'Perfume Delight'
'Sheer Bliss'
'Showbiz'
'Summer Fashion'
'Sutter's Gold'
'Tiffany'
'Voodoo'

OTHER SCENTED PLANTS

Cestrum nocturnum, night-blooming jasmine
Citrus, orange blossoms
Convallaria majalis, lily of the valley
Daphne odora, daphne
Gardenia jasminoides, gardenia
Heliotropium arborescens, heliotrope
Ipomoea alba, moonflower
Lathyrus odoratus, sweet pea
Lavandula angustifolia, lavender
Lonicera japonica 'Halliana', Hall's honeysuckle
Paeonia sp., herbaceous peony
Rhododendron 'Fragrantissimum', R. 'King George'
Trachelospermum jasminoides, star jasmine
Wisteria sinensis, Chinese wisteria

"Borrowing" Scenery

Attractive plantings in neighboring yards can be "borrowed" by planting smaller versions of the same species on the garden perimeter, thereby giving your landscape the illusion of added depth.

Designers of Oriental-style landscapes often utilize neighboring shrubs and trees to visually expand a garden. If there are handsome, mature trees in an adjacent yard, a nearby planting of smaller trees of the same species in your garden will create an illusion of depth, a continuing vista.

This same principle can be applied to achieve effective windbreaks and to enhance privacy screening. Evaluate the neighboring vegetation and incorporate it into your overall landscape scheme—you will enhance the general view and produce a sense of continuity.

Distant views that offer pleasant vistas can also be captured by "framing" them with structures or plantings. Chinese moongates are excellent for this purpose. On approaching the gate, the viewer is presented with a panorama beyond almost as a framed painting. We have seen many Portland, Oregon, gardeners use this technique to adopt Mount Hood as their own personal vista, glimpsed through artfully designed windows in lattice screens and garden walls or flanked by Douglas firs.

SHARING SCENERY

Scenery can also be shared with like-minded neighbors. In developments or areas where individual yards open onto a common greenspace, it is often possible, and desirable, to redesign the greenbelt to create a safer place for children to play or to merely enhance the landscape to achieve a more appealing vista for all. The added benefit is that a well-designed central greenspace draws the eye away from individual gardens.

In many urban areas, where yards can be tiny and fences constricting, walls are not used to define property lines. Instead, neighbors opt to open their yards onto a common greenbelt that is shared as one flowing outdoor space by all the families who live on the block. Children have a vast, parklike environment for their games and everyone contributes to its upkeep.

These changes require the cooperation of neighbors united to attain a common goal and may involve legal considerations, particularly when homeowner associations are involved, but problems can be solved with this spirit of cooperation. One group of homeowners joined forces to plant a row of screening trees to hide a string of overhead power lines erected by the local utility company. In another city, homeowners united to erect a wall between backyards and block a coastal access walk that attracted rowdy students from a nearby college on weekends. The wall, while not high enough to block views, measurably increased the homeowners' privacy.

The concept of borrowing scenery is classically demonstrated in this scene. By keeping the perimeter plantings low, the designer of this seductive garden included the stately old trees in the adjacent yard into the overall view from the patio. The fortunate owners of the garden shown have the benefit of the trees without the responsibility of maintaining them.

CHAPTER SIX

Redesigning the Garden
case studies

I have banished all worldly care
from my garden; it is a clean and
open spot.

—Hsieh Ling-Yin, 410 A.D.

Far right: This inviting garden demonstrates the delightful result of careful planning and design. An integrated design, it nevertheless offers several different destinations, including a deck, a gazebo retreat, an adjacent cookout area, and ample room to entertain guests.

Well into the twentieth century, residential landscape designs were conceived as showcases for neighbors and passersby to admire and, perhaps, envy. Front yards were for display (no one ever actually used them) and backyards for family activities or the cultivation of a few flower beds. The results of this type of thinking can be seen at many of the old estates whose manor houses are surrounded by gardens no one ever ventures into, save the gardeners who maintain them. Even many suburban gardeners bought into the idea, manicuring their front lawns and foundation plantings into perfect facades designed to instill envy in less talented neighbors, while tending a couple of rosebushes in the backyard amid a sea of less well-kept grass.

To some extent, the front yard will always be for display. But as we have seen, with creative gardeners taking back their front spaces for private use and rethinking their back and side yards, it is safe to say that a revolution in garden use is taking place.

As a renaissance of gardening has swept across the continent and as gardening stores, catalogs, and magazines have sprung up, gardens across the country are being redesigned as private spaces that provide a range of activites not previously associated with gardening. Garden lovers have begun to incorporate amenities that were once found mainly in civic facilities, private clubs, or public gardens—from tennis courts to outdoor kitchens and from elegant swimming pools and spas to complex fountains and water gardens.

Before you undertake a redesign of your yard to create your private Eden, consider the goal(s) you want to reach as the garden matures. Ask yourself if the features you want now are likely to be the ones you will want in five or ten years.

For example, a play area is essential to families with children, but once the children have grown, there is no longer a need for an elaborate play center. With this eventuality in mind, these spaces should be designed so that they can easily be converted to other uses when the time arrives.

A swimming pool is a costly undertaking and gobbles up considerable space. Unless the adults in the family intend to use the pool regularly during the year, it might be more practical to downsize the project to a lap or exercise pool—a growing trend in America.

One couple who had an Olympic-size pool installed when their children were small ultimately converted it to a gargantuan koi pond once the children left home. We have met a number of couples who eventually filled in their pool and transformed the space into an island garden or lawn.

Any yard or garden project that involves pouring a concrete slab should be carefully weighed as to its suitability in the years to come. It is expensive and difficult to remove an expanse of concrete several inches thick. Bricks or other paving laid in sand are often just as suitable and much less troublesome to dismantle should this be desired or necessary down the road.

Most people who garden are confident of their ability to glean dazzling results from their efforts. As the old Chinese proverb wryly observes, "All gardeners know better than other gardeners." But unless one has had some experience in redesigning a landscape, it is advisable to consult with a professional garden designer or even a landscape architect. These experts have the training and, usually, the experience to propose solutions and options you may not have considered. They also have the technical expertise to know what is practicable and what is not, as well as what is needed to solve problems such as

ensuring proper drainage and achieving specific design goals. Oftentimes,
a designer will oversee the work, even
hiring the craftspeople and labor to
bring the plan to fruition.

Probably the best way to grasp
the possibilities in one's own landscape is to share the experiences
others have had in designing their
outdoor spaces. Following are case
histories (together with plans and
photographs) of families who have
successfully pursued their dreams of
creating privacy, elegance, and usefulness in their gardens and found that,
as Ann Scott-James observed, "There
is more pleasure in making a garden
than in contemplating a paradise."
One thing that will soon become
apparent is that nearly all of those
whose gardens are included had well-
defined ideas of what they wanted
and took a hands-on approach, even
when they retained a professional
designer. This active involvement,
they said, ensured that their goals
would be met and that the resulting
design would serve their needs.

Case Study One

Conquering a Difficult Site

*I*t was the lot that had captivated Peter and Teri—a precipitous slope overlooking an untamed canyon where wildlife roamed without fear of humans.

Construction of the house and the garden required some feats of engineering to anchor them to the declivity. Several cubic yards of soil and rock had to be removed to provide a practicable building site. Installing the various outdoor spaces would be another challenge.

Achieving privacy was a major consideration for the owners. "While the land was pretty much pristine, there were other homes nearby and a number of others were under construction," Peter recalled. "We knew that, eventually, we would have a privacy problem as the density increased." This was exacerbated by the fact that the sunken site lay several feet below the street and was exposed on two sides to public view from overlooking terrain.

To develop the garden, he consulted with landscape designer Ken Coverdell, who had created other residential landscapes in the area. Because of the difficult site, there was space for only a large side yard garden. The rear of the proper-

ty abutted a ledge that dropped off to the canyon floor some one hundred feet (30m) below.

There was certainly no room for a swimming pool if there was to be a garden of any consequence, yet the owners had their hearts set on one. A solution was found by reevaluating the idea of where a pool should be sited and realizing that in this case, the best spot was *under* the rear portion of the house, which rested on columns and beams. So that the pool could be used all year and to maximize privacy, it was built as a natatorium with glass walls on three sides. A deck was cantilevered over the canyon at one end, accessible from the pool through sliding glass doors.

Since Peter is an avid gardener, he involved himself in selecting the plant palette, which ultimately included more than fifty different shrubs, trees, and perennials—a selection that ensured that something of interest would be visible in the garden in all seasons.

Tall-growing shrubs and trees were the first to be planted, since they would serve as background and screening material around the perimeter of the garden. Island beds of ferns and perennials followed, placed around a flagstone patio that was interplanted with groundcover capable of withstanding foot traffic.

Peter and Teri designed this garden from scratch, laying a flagstone patio to fill the side yard and setting flower beds into it. A deck was added to provide an area for outdoor cooking and dining.

Peter and Teri enjoyed frequent family gatherings and entertaining, so they decided to build a redwood deck and outdoor kitchen with a double cooktop barbecue. For stealing quiet moments away from the crowds, they decided to add a gazebo.

Over the last three years, the garden has matured into a magical and totally private retreat with lush vegetation and color on many levels.

1. Deciduous trees, including Chinese pistache (*Pistachia chinensis*) and ginkgo (*Ginkgo biloba*)
2. Evergreen trees and shrubs, including black pine (*Pinus nigra*), Monterey pine (*P. radiata*), Swiss mountain pine (*P. mugo*), redwood (*Sequoia sempervirens*), sweet bay (*Laurus nobilis*), strawberry tree (*Arbutus unedo*), camellia (*C. japonica*), wild lilac (*Ceanothus 'Concha'*), flannel bush (*Fremontodendron californicum*), grevillea (*G. 'Noellii'*), and pittosporum (*P. eugenioides*)
3. Bedding plants, including fornight lily (*Dietes iridioides*), star jasmine (*Trachelospermum jasminoides*), red salvia (*Salvia coccinea*), sage (*Salvia officinalis*), impatiens (*I. wallerana*), candytuft (*Iberis sempervirens*), snapdragon (*Antirrhinum majus*), floss flower (*Ageratum houstonianum*), and big blue lily turf (*Liriope muscari*)
4. Stairway
5. Deck
6. Gazebo

Case Study Two

Utilitarian Structures Can Be Landscape Assets

This landscape remodeling of a small front yard shows how structures and plant material can be combined to create a handsome, private space. Virtually every feature shown is an addition to the old landscape.

on and Wendy purchased a home in Portland, Oregon, that possessed only a modest setback from a busy residential thoroughfare. They soon realized that some provision would need to be made for achieving privacy, especially since the master bedroom faced the street.

"Headlights flashed through the bedroom at night, even with the drapes drawn. In addition, we felt exposed whenever we sat on our bedroom deck," Wendy recalled. "Because the front yard is so small, we didn't want to imprison ourselves behind a high fence or hedge, but we wanted to feel a bit more protected from public view."

Their Portland landscape architect, John Herbst, Jr., devised a solution that involved structures that appear to be fences, but are broken up so that they do not create an enclosed compound effect.

A streetside screen was designed with vertical louvers that were installed at an angle that gives the owners a view of the street but blocks street views into the yard. From the street, the screen appears to be a camouflaged carport.

At the entry, Herbst designed a novel multiuse structure that cleverly blocks views from the street to the deck and bedroom; the garden-tool storage cabinet with hidden double doors is topped by a planter with a tin-lined cavity that houses plants. The cabinet not only serves as an attractive sight screen but also defines the entry, directing guests to the front door.

Both structures were detailed and stained to match the residence so that they appear to be part of the original architectural design.

"John strategically placed evergreen shrubs in the openings between the structures that give us additional privacy without making us feel like we're imprisoned," Wendy observed.

1. Japanese maple *(Acer palmatum)*
2. Douglas fir *(Pseudotsuga menziesii)*
3. Japanese camellia *(C. japonica)*
4. Barberry *(Berberis* sp.*)*

5. Entry deck
6. Entry walk
7. Sightscreen

Case Study Three

Privacy in Cramped Quarters

Trees and tall-growing shrubs provide a living screen that is much more appealing to the eye than a fence or wall. The courtyard walls were kept low so that family members could view the garden beyond from their lounge chairs.

*M*ost urban neighborhoods suffer from a common problem—density. It is a challenge to wrest some privacy from a city yard, but it can be done.

Kevin and Destiny's ranch-style home in Los Angeles is located at the end of a cul-de-sac. The front yard was exposed and the rear yard was narrow and open to view from neighbors' windows that are only a few feet away.

Landscape architect Lani Berrington conceived a solution for reclaiming and bringing privacy to the front yard. On the portion near the street, she built up a berm that provided an elevated site for planting screening shrubs and trees. This opened up the opportunity to use part of the front yard for outdoor living space, a desirable goal given that there was so little rear yard.

A brick courtyard with a low wall and entry gate replaced what was once foundation beds and a lawn area, although the design left a substantial buffer of lawn and entry walk from the courtyard to the street. To muffle traffic noise and provide some visual diversion, a raised koi pond set at seating height and featuring a recirculating fountain as the focal point was installed in the courtyard using the same brick that made up the floor and walls.

In the rear, she tackled the privacy issue by planting a screening row of timber bamboo fronted by leafy tree ferns to block the neighbors' view without making Destiny and Kevin feel imprisoned. To enhance the very narrow yard, into which the previous owners had simply laid a concrete walk, she laid a brick path over the concrete and installed

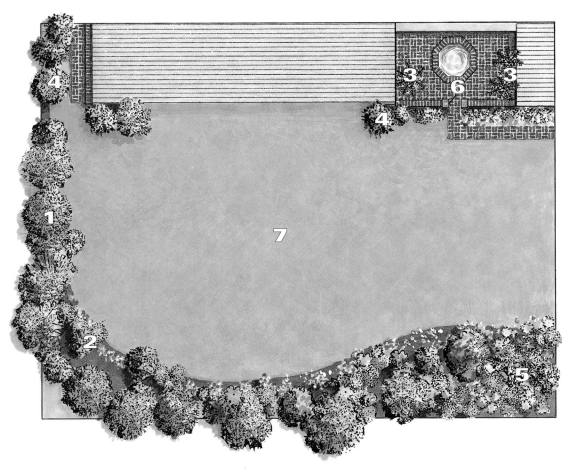

an L-shaped lily pond, giving the yard a sense of movement despite its diminutive size.

"We hardly ever stepped out back before," Destiny noted, but now the renovated yards, back and front, are in almost continual use for informal dining, relaxing, and entertaining.

1. California sycamore (*Plantanus racemosa*)
2. Brush cherry (*Syzygium paniculatum*)
3. Australian tree fern (*Cyathea cooperi*)
4. Bronze loquat (*Eribotrya deflexa*)
5. Bedding plants including lily-of-the-Nile (*Agapanthus orientalis*), busy Lizzie (*Impatiens wallerana*), and sweet alyssum (*Lobularia maritima*)
6. Courtyard patio and koi pond
7. Lawn (*'Marathon'* turf grass)

Case Study Four

Good Design Can Solve Landscape Problems

How does one re-configure a long, narrow yard so that it is more functional and appealing? By establishing inti-mate spaces within it. Here, trellises and arbors serve as walls for smaller rooms that are keyed to specific uses.

*D*ebra and Phillip fell in love with the brick Colonial builder "spec" house, but the backyard had some problems. The house was the only one left among several in an upscale development. It had languished on the market for nearly two years because it had what seemed to be insoluble drainage problems caused by the natural topography of the land, and, worst of all, it commanded a view of a phalanx of high-tension towers in the distance that, in addition to being a blot on the landscape, hummed ominously like a plague of metalbeasts.

With the idea in mind that a good garden designer could transform the outdoor space into a private sanctuary and solve the view and drainage problems, they consulted with landscape architect Michael Glassman, who had a reputation among their friends for turning ugly duck-lings into swans. His assurances that the dif-ficulties were surmountable convinced them to buy the house.

Glassman's first step was to install a complex drainage system. Not only did it channel the natural runoff underground and into a sewer line, but the system also worked to benefit the plantings by collect-ing irrigation water from beds and planters he designed.

Next, he specified a wall of conifers fronted by lower-growing plant material

along the back property line that would, in less than two years, completely block the view of the electrical towers, filter out noise, and obscure the yard from view from neighboring homes.

To screen the remaining sides, Glassman designed trellises and trellised fencing that, when softened with evergreen vines, would enclose the space yet would not overpower it. Color would come from a series of raised bed planters encircling the perimeter. Finally, as the owners requested, off the master suite he designed a sheltered and screened retreat with a waterfall.

A few years have lapsed since the owners first glimpsed the house that would be their home. Viewing snapshots of the virgin, desolate rear yard, they still marvel at the transformation.

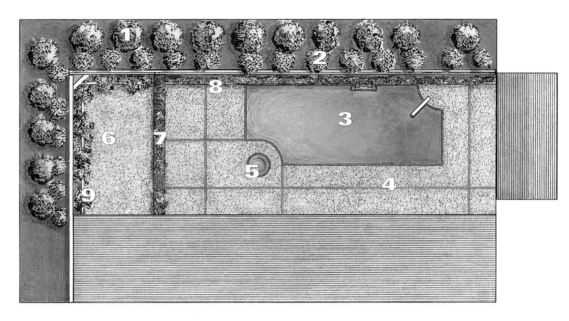

1. Bay tree *(Laurus nobilis)*
2. Leyland cypress *(cupressocyparis leylandii)*
3. Swimming pool
4. Patio
5. Spa
6. Secluded patio
7. Trellis with climbing roses
8. Rose *(Rosa* sp.*)* and Japanese pittosporum *(P. tobira)* in planter
9. Japanese maple *(Acer palmatum)*

Case Study Five

Privacy without Fences or Walls

Breaking with tradition, the designer eliminated all the clichés in this delightful front yard landscape, discarding fences, gates, lawn—even the conventional front entry access.

*N*orma and Peter wanted more privacy for the entry and front facade of their home, which was visible from the street, but they didn't want to install a fence, wall, or other obstruction. They had ruled out a hedge, which would not be appropriate for the architectural theme of their house.

Several consultations with the Sacramento landscape design firm of Environmental Creations, Inc., produced an interesting and privacy-oriented landscape plan. Instead of an entry walk that extended in a straight line from the public sidewalk to the front door, there would be a stepped bridge over a koi pond that approached the house at an angle.

In keeping with the lodge theme, dwarf and standard conifers would be used with ferns and deciduous material, such as Japanese maple *(Acer palmatum)*, not only to replicate the woodsy feeling the owners sought to achieve, but also to screen windows from direct view.

"The effect we were looking for was an informal front yard with a pond similar to lakes you might find in the woods, surrounded by rock outcroppings and native plants," Norma recalled. "It really takes a season or two for plants to grow in so everything looks natural instead of man-made—in fact, the more years that pass, the better a garden looks."

1. Japanese maple *(Acer palmatum)*
2. Tasmanian tree fern *(Dicksonia antarctica)*
3. Coast redwood *(Sequoia sempervirens)*
4. Saucer magnolia *(M. soulangeana)*
5. Fern bed (various species)
6. Entry walk
7. Koi pond
8. Entry

Case Study Six

At Home in the Woods

*I*t was a challenge for Pamela and John to save as many of the lofty trees on their lot in Lake Oswego, Oregon, as they ultimately were able to do. The contractor

who built their home explained to them the difficulty of maneuvering heavy equipment and trucks around the mature trees on the site and wanted to remove several to create an open pad.

By negotiation and cajoling, and working with their landscape architect, the owners were able to preserve all but seven trees. While it was unfortunate that some trees had to be sacrificed, they took comfort in the knowledge that they could plant new specimens once the house was built.

Instead of a direct route from the street to the site, construction traffic took a serpentine route around several

Wood, with its warmth and beauty, has many applications in the residential landscape. Foremost among these is in the construction of decks. Here, one may see how versatile decks can be, serving as a front entry, a foundation for a spa, an outdoor family room, and an elevated retreat for sunning or viewing the garden.

towering firs—a fact that distressed no one but the contractor.

"Interestingly enough," Pamela said, "the contractor eventually came around to our way of thinking and began to refer to the firs as 'our trees.'"

Despite the fact that the site was, for the most part, wilderness, there were adjacent neighbors. The owners' concept was to carve out a semi-wild, pristine-looking retreat in the backyard. Rather than clear out vegetation to create pads for decks and other amenities, their intention was to fit these elements into the native terrain as much as possible.

Their landscape architect proposed a combination of screening walls and plant material to achieve maximum privacy around sunning decks and a spa that would be installed in the center of the rear deck. By blending similar shrubs, trees, and vines with indigenous flora around the structures, they appeared to be embraced by their surroundings, rather than intruding on them.

"We have seen the landscape grow in around the decks and over the walls so that everything seems to be in harmony," Pamela observed. "This was our original goal."

1. Douglas fir *(Pseudotsuga menziesii)*
2. Schwedler maple *(Acer platanoides 'Schwedleri')*
3. Azalea *(Rhododendron* sp.*)*
4. Evergreen clematis *(Clematis armandii)*

5. Spa deck
6. Upper deck
7. Sunning deck

Case Study Seven

A Grand Garden Continues to Evolve

Years of tending and maturation are required for a garden to reach its peak of perfection, and this one—in Falls Church, Virginia, one of the most alluring gardens we have seen—is testament to this fact.

Owners James and Mary have expanded the plantings over several years and added amenities that have made the outdoor spaces more useful. James grew up on the property and had an enduring love for the towering trees and dazzling azaleas that were planted and nurtured over the decades by his parents. When he acquired the property in the 1980s, he installed serpentine walks of stone that wend their way through the shrubs and trees, luring one deeper into the bowers and byways to discover hidden delights.

Over the years, additional layers of perimeter plantings have been added to screen the garden and create a comforting sense of privacy in what appears to be a grand English manor house garden.

A great part of what makes the garden magnificent is the well-conceived but seemingly casual mix of coniferous and broadleaf material, both deciduous and evergreen. Included are Alberta spruce, Japanese maple, lilac, boxwood, azalea, mahonia, and a delightful selection of perennials and groundcovers.

Tucked out of view and awaiting discovery by guests strolling through the trees is an elegant Williamsburg-style garden structure (we refuse to call it a shed) that provides extravagant storage for yard maintenance equipment.

Perched on a hillock surrounded by floral splendor and greenery is a terrace that commands a 360-degree

panorama of the grounds. Below this, sequestered from view, is a nook with seating that serves as a getaway for reading or merely resting in the garden.

Scattered among the plantings and sculpture are birdhouses and a lilac-encircled dovecote that attracts avian visitors through the seasons.

"Our family has been adding to and enhancing the garden for close to sixty years," James observed, "but we still consider it a work in progress."

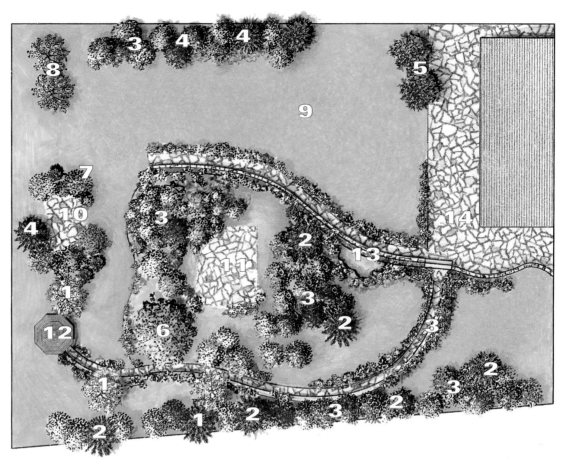

1. Eastern dogwood *(Cornus florida)*	8. Lilac *(Syringa vulgaris)*
2. Alberta spruce *(Picea glauca)*	9. Lawn (mixed fescue turf)
3. Azalea *(Rhododendron* sp.*)*	10. Hidden patio
4. Longleaf pine *(P. palustris)*	11. Hilltop patio
5. Japanese maple *(Acer palmatum)*	12. Garden tool storage
6. Oak *(Quercus* sp.*)*	13. Pool and waterfall
7. Boxwood *(Buxus* sp.*)*	14. Flagstone patio

Case Study Eight

A Herculean Renovation

Here is proof that an exceptional back yard need not be spacious to be stunning. It has all the ingredients needed for a private retreat, including a level plane for casual outdoor dining, ample trees for shade, a pool and fountain for music, and legions of blooming plants for beauty and aroma.

Anyone who has commenced a wholesale revamping of a landscape or garden knows that it is not an easy task to change the natural profile of the land and—if such a project is undertaken—to do so with successful results. Helen and Phillip embarked on just such a venture a few years ago when they sought to create a shadier and less exposed rear garden at their suburban home.

They designed a gently sloping hillside garden with exposed rocks and a steep waterfall that would introduce the soothing sound of moving water into their proposed retreat. Careful positioning of pathways and steps was necessary to create access for maintenance. Helen and Phillip wanted to create summer shade for the patio below, so they chose specific locations to add trees and shrubs, which also provided screening as they matured along the boundary fenceline.

To bring the design to fruition, they imported 16 tons (14.5t) of topsoil and 17 tons (15.5t) of rock. Once these were in place, trees, shrubs, perennials, and bulbs were planted following the plan created by Phillip, who is a noted floral designer. Included in the palette are azalea, holly, weeping cedar, cypress, redbud, dogwood, and a kaleidoscope of bulbs, perennials, and groundcovers.

Where there was once an uninspiring and mundane backyard, open to view and the unrelenting rays of the summer sun, there now is a cool, secluded haven that draws the owners outdoors to enjoy the sights and sounds of their personal oasis without providing a show for the neighbors.

As with most renovation projects, Helen and Phillip learned that one must triple the estimated time required to complete such a project and double the projected cost.

"Although it was a lot of work and mess, the result was worth all the inconvenience," Phillip observed. "We use the garden much more often than we did before. Our only regret is that we didn't do this sooner."

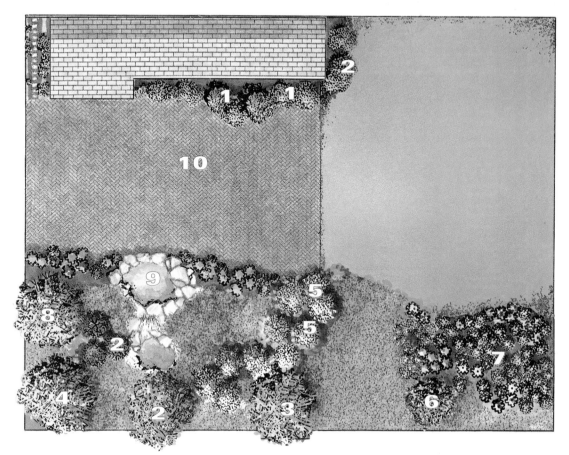

1. Burford holly *(Ilex cornuta 'Burfordii')*
2. Azalea *(Rhododendron sp.)*
3. Sweet gum *(Liquidambar styraciflua)*
4. Cypress *(Cupressus sp.)*
5. Eastern dogwood *(Cornus florida)*
6. Eastern redbud *(Cercis canadensis)*
7. Bedding plants including bulbs, hosta, Japanese painted fern *(Athyrium nipponicum* 'Pictum'*)*, and a variety of annuals and perennials
8. Weeping cedar *(Cedrus atlantica 'Pendula')*
9. Waterfall and pool
10. Patio

The beauty of brick, particularly very old masonry, in the garden is masterfully demonstrated in this small garden in Charleston, South Carolina. Greenery draped across the walls helps soften the impact of so much brick in such an abbreviated space.

Case Study Nine

Reconfiguring a Historic Garden

The city of Charleston, South Carolina, is generally acknowledged as the cradle of genteel Southern life. Its old town section includes many sites of historical interest as well as elegant restaurants and shops.

Only a block removed on either side of Meeting and King streets, two of the city's major commercial thoroughfares, are the city's residential architectural treasures—historic homes that, in many cases, date from colonial times when Charles Towne was founded in 1670. Except for some landmark estate homes, they are densely concentrated because the demand for building lots always exceeded the supply. This tightly packed collection of historic homes creates a charming ambiance but makes the quest for privacy an elusive goal. The result has been the evolution of a city of quaint walled gardens and courtyards, which has proven to be an irrisistible lure for droves of tourists eager for a peek inside. This curiosity, in turn, has prompted some residents to add even greater height to the barriers around their property.

It was a need for more space and a desire to revitalize the garden that motivated the owners of one of these walled havens to consult landscape architects Hugh Dargan and Mary Palmer Dargan, who are experts in the field of historic garden restoration.

Renovations in the antiquarian section are closely watched by the Historic Charleston Foundation and the Center for Historic Preservation. Within the limitations placed on the remodeling by the historic preservation entities, the Dargans developed a plan that would open up the space but leave no telltale footprint.

First, a small outbuilding (called a "necessary" in the South) was razed and the bricks from the demolition were used to construct a double-arched wall that effectively divided the yard into two garden rooms. The late European masonry craftsman Hugo Tezza constructed the new wall and wedded it to the existing brick structures so expertly that even a careful examination does not reveal where new leaves off and old begins.

A trellis on which vines are trained was installed over a section of the garden to fashion an outdoor dining room—something the owners had wanted for intimate outdoor dinner parties.

This new configuration gave the owners an elegant space that could accommodate up to 250 guests when the French doors to the house were opened.

Existing plantings included a three-decades-old Lady Banks rose, as well as English ivy that provided a lush mantle for the brick walls. Added to these were clematis, mahonia, variegated lace-cap hydrangea, *Fatsia japonica*, and ferns.

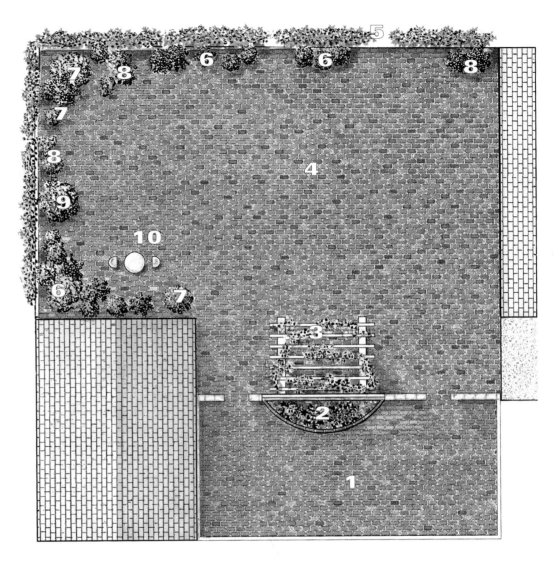

1. Outer patio
2. Planter containing lamb's ears (*Stachys byzantina*), daylily (*Hemerocallis* sp.), herbs, lavender (*Lavandula* sp.), spotted nettle (*Lamium maculatum*), and dusty miller (*Senecio cineraria*)
3. Trellis with wisteria (*Wisteria sinensis*)
4. Inner patio
5. Lady Banks rose (*Rosa banksiae*) and English ivy (*Hedera helix*)
6. Lacecap hydrangea (*Hydrangea macrophylla* 'Maculata')
7. Mahonia (*M. aquifolium*)
8. Ferns (various species)
9. Japanese fatsia (*Fatsia japonica*)
10. Seating area

Case Study Ten

Taming a Slope for Family Use

Panoramic views and an illusion of woodsy suburbia have drawn residents to the hills of Brentwood, California, since the 1920s. It provides a pastoral environment within a stone's throw of one of the nation's populous and paved-over cities—Los Angeles.

Richard and Susan bought their old estate home here several years ago, knowing it and the garden needed considerable renovation after several years of neglect. Once the restorative work on the house was completed, they focused on the yard.

Their goals included adding a swimming pool, replacing the minuscule and deteriorated patio, and transforming a steep slope of native vegetation into a usable extension of the rear yard.

They retained the firm of Nick Williams & Associates to help them achieve their goals. Award-winning designer Nick Williams had helped some of their neighbors solve knotty landscape problems and they liked his approach, which was to use natural materials wherever possible and to adapt a plan to the terrain, rather than the reverse.

A large patio of bouquet canyon stone replaced the small original, but the stone salvaged from its demolition was recycled into planters and other amenities. The pool was designed to simulate a lagoon, with large boulders and river cobble placed around much of the coping to soften the hard edges of the paving stone.

To conquer the steep slope at the rear of the property, a winding path was cut into the acclivity and timber steps laid. River cobble was used to create retainers along the flight of steps and these were interplanted with annuals, perennials, creeping groundcover, and ferns. Added to the native flora on the slope were acacia, pine, and pittosporum trees and ceanothus shrubs.

Commanding a view of the Brentwood hills on the crest of the slope is a new gazebo that provides a pleasant and scenic spot for enjoying the garden and relaxing in the benign southern California climate most of the year. The owners often have Sunday breakfast here while they pore over newspapers.

Susan recalled how it was before: "We often looked up the hill longingly and discussed how nice it would be to have our own little private jungle retreat up there and be able to use all of our property. We use it a lot now and the kids spend a lot of time exploring and playing up there with their friends."

1. Hilltop gazebo
2. India hawthorn *(Rhaphiolepis indica)*
3. Aleppo pine *(P. halepensis)*
4. Jacaranda *(J. mimosifolia)*
5. Sword fern *(Polystichum munitum)*
6. California sycamore *(Platanus racemosa)*
7. Swimming pool
8. Flagstone patio
9. Victorian box *(Pittosporum undulatum)*

Sources

Garden Accents

Anderson Design
P.O. Box 4057 C
Bellingham, WA 98227
800-947-7697
Arbors, trellises, gates, and pyramids (Oriental, modern, and traditional styles)

Bamboo Fencer
31 Germania Street
Jamaica Plain, Boston, MA 02130
617-524-6137
Free brochure; $3 catalog (refundable)
Bamboo fences

Boston Turning Works
42 Plymouth Street
Boston, MA 02118
617-482-9085
$1 for brochure
Distinctive wood finials for gates, fenceposts, and balustrades

Brooks Barrel Company
P.O. Box 1056
Cambridge, MD 21613-1046
410-228-0790
$2 for brochure
Natural-finish pine wooden barrels and planters

Charleston Gardens
61 Queen Street
Charleston, SC 29401
803-723-0252
$3 catalog

Florentine Craftsmen Inc.
46-24 28th Street
Long Island City, NY 11101
718-937-7632
Garden furniture, ornaments, fountains and statuary of lead, stone, and bronze

Flower Framers by Jay
671 Wilmer Avenue
Cincinnati, Ohio 45226
Flower boxes

FrenchWyres
P.O. Box 131655
Tyler, TX 75713
903-597-8322
$4 catalog
Wire garden furnishings: trellis, urns, cachepots, window boxes, arches, and plant stands

Gardensheds
651 Millcross Road
Lancaster, PA 17601
$4 for brochure
Potting sheds, wood boxes, and larger storage units

Hooks Lattice
7949 Silverton Avenue #903
San Diego, CA 92126
800-896-0978
Free catalog
Wrought-iron gardenware

Kenneth Lynch & Sons
84 Danbury Road
P.O. Box 488
Wilton, CT 06897
203-762-8363
Free brochure
Benches, gates, scupture and statuary, planters and urns, topiary, sundials, and weathervanes

Kinsman Company
River Road
Point Pleasant, PA 18950
800-733-4146
Free catalog
European plant supports, pillars, arches trellises, flowerpots, and planters

Lake Creek Garden Features Inc.
P.O. Box 118
Lake City, IA 51449
712-464-8924
Free brochure
Obelisks, plant stands, and gazing globes and stands

Liteform Designs
P.O. Box 3316
Portland, OR 97208
503-253-1210
Garden lighting: path, bullard, accent, step, and tree fixtures

New Blue Moon Studio
P.O. Box 579
Leavenworth, WA 98826
509-548-4754
Trellises, gates, arbors, and garden furniture

New England Garden Ornaments
P.O. Box 235
38 East Brookfield Road
North Brookfield, MA 01535
508-867-4474
Free brochure, $8 for catalog
Garden fountains and statuary, planters and urns, antique furniture, sundials, and limestone ornaments

Stone Forest
P.O. Box 2840
Sante Fe, NM 87504
505-986-8883
Hand-carved granite birdbaths, basins, fountains, lanterns, and spheres

Tanglewood Conservatories
Silver Spring, MD
Free brochure
Handcrafted period glass houses and atriums

Tidewater Workshop
Oceanville, NJ 08231
800-666-8433
Free catalog
White cedar benches, chairs, swings, and tables

Valcovic Cornell Design
Box 380
Beverly, MA 01915
$4 for catalog, redeemable with purchase
Trellises and arbor benches (traditional and contemporary styles)

Vixen Hill Manufacturing Company
Main Street
Elverson, PA 19520
800-423-2766
Cedar gazebos and screened garden houses

Weatherend Estate Furniture
6 Gordon Drive
Rockland, ME 04841
800-456-6483
Heirloom-quality garden furniture

Seeds and Plants

Bear Creek Nursery
PO Box 411
Northport, WA 99157
Specializes in cold-hardy fruit trees, shrubs, and berries, many of them ideal for wildlife.

Forestfarm
990 Tetherow Road
Williams, OR 97544
(503) 846-7269
Catalog of more than 2000 plants, including Western natives, perennials, and an outstanding variety of trees and shrubs.

The Fragrant Path
PO Box 328
Ft. Calhoun, NE 68023
Seeds for fragrant annuals, perennials, shrubs, and vines, many of them old-fashioned favorites.

Lilypons Water Gardens
PO Box 10
6800 Lilypons Road
Buckeystown, MD 21717
(301) 874-5133
Plants and supplies for water gardens.

Niche Gardens
1111 Dawson Rd.
Chapel Hill, NC 27516
(919) 967-0078

Grasses, nursery-propagated wildflowers, perennials, and herbs.

Northwoods Nursery
27368 South Oglesby
Canby, OR 97013
503-266-5432
Free catalog and growing guide
Nursery features, ornamental trees, shrubs, and vines

Prairie Moon Nursery
Rt. 3 Box 163
Winona, MN 55987
(507) 452-1362
Generously sized plants, seeds of native prairie grasses and wildflowers.

Shady Oaks Nursery
112 10th Ave. SE
Waseca, MN 56093
(507) 835-5033
Specializes in plants that thrive in shade, including wildflowers, ferns, perennials, shrubs, and others.

Tripple Brook Farm
37 Middle Rd.
Southampton, MA 01073
(413) 527-4626
Catalog featuring wildflowers, Northeastern native plants, fruits, and shrubs.

Van Ness Water Gardens
2460 N. Euclid Ave.
Upland, CA 91786
(909) 982-2425
Everything for a water garden, from plants to pools to supplies.

Wayside Gardens
1 Garden Lane
Hodges, SC 29695-0001
Free catalog
Worldwide ornamental garden plants, hardy bulbs

Yucca Do Nursery
PO Box 655
Waller, TX 77484
(409) 826-6363

Wide selection of trees, shrubs, and perennial plants, including many natives.

Canadian Plant Sources

Corn Hill Nursery Ltd.
RR 5
Petitcodiac NB EOA 2HO

Ferncliff Gardens
SS 1
Mission, British Columbia
V2V 5V6

McFayden Seed Co. Ltd.
Box 1800
Brandon, Manitoba
R7A 6N4

Stirling Perennials
RR 1
Morpeth, Ontario
N0P 1X0

Australian Plant Sources

Country Farm Perennials
RSD Laings Road
Nayook VIC 3821

Cox's Nursery
RMB 216 Oaks Road
Thrilmere NSW 2572

Honeysuckle Cottage Nursery
Lot 35 Bowen Mountain Road
Bowen Mountain via Grosevale NSW 2753

Swan Bros Pty Ltd
490 Galston Road
Dural NSW 2158

Index